HEADLESS BODY IN TOPLESS BAR

HEADLESS BODY IN TOPLESS BAR

THE BEST HEADLINES FROM AMERICA'S FAVORITE NEWSPAPER

The Staff of *The New York Post*

HarperEntertainment

An Imprint of HarperCollinsPublishers

HEADLESS BODY IN TOPLESS BAR. Copyright © 2007 by The New York Post. All rights reserved. Printed in the United States of America. No part of this book may be used or reproduced in any manner whatsoever without written permission except in the case of brief quotations embodied in critical articles and reviews. For information address HarperCollins Publishers, 10 East 53rd Street, New York, NY 10022.

HarperCollins books may be purchased for educational, business, or sales promotional use. For information please write: Special Markets Department, HarperCollins Publishers, 10 East 53rd Street, New York, NY 10022.

FIRST EDITION

Designed by Renato Stanisic

Library of Congress Cataloging-in-Publication Data

Headless body in topless bar : the best headlines from America's favorite newspaper / The Staff of the New York Post.
    p. cm.
  ISBN 978-0-06-134071-0
 1. New York Post 2. Newspapers—Headlines—Humor.
  PN4899.N42P68 2007
  071'.471—dc22

2007032853

08 09 10 11 12 ov/rrd 10 9 8 7 6 5 4 3 2 1

SECTIONS

PREFACE

Before any discussion of *New York Post* headlines, one should paraphrase what E.B. White once wrote about humor: You can dissect a joke as you would a frog, but like the frog, it tends to die on the table.

That said, there are common threads throughout these pages. At its best, a *Post* headline has attitude and guts. And it certainly doesn't hesitate to employ humor if the story calls for it (and sometimes, as some critics assert, when it doesn't).

It wasn't always so. Back in the day, *Post* heads were as staid and conventional as any other paper's (save, perhaps, the eternally stolid *Times*).

What made the difference? When were we granted leave to be wacky?

It had to be the Australians and the Brits.

There is no other way to explain the sea change that occurred after Dorothy Schiff sold *The Post* to Rupert Murdoch in 1976. Headlines rapidly shifted from the pedestrian and institutional to the rollicking and attitudinal.

Murdoch imported his version of the Best and the Brightest, and the sagging and lethargic *Post* of the late Dolly years got a serious shot of adrenaline.

People like Steve Dunleavy (still with us and also a pub called Langan's), Neil Travis (who created Page Six out of whole cloth) and Roger Wood covered New York City in a way the competition hadn't in a very long time—that is, as a new and exciting metropolis.

And this crew also put the other papers on notice that A.) There was a new genus of journalism in town, and B.) Readers would be allowed to enjoy themselves as they consumed it.

That enterprising spirit survived Murdoch's ownership hiatus (1988–1993) and the chaos that ensued, and the same spirit was revivified upon his return.

It is present still under Editor-in-Chief Col Allan—he believes a lot of other newspapers still miss the point entirely.

"Clearly, our first responsibility is to inform in a comprehensive manner," says Allan. "But as important, we must engage the reader—or we lose the reader, which obviates the first point. The competition doesn't seem to get that."

As for "over-the-top" headlines, Allan returns to the same theme.

"We're delighted when the headlines entertain. Remember, the very purpose of the head-line is to draw the readers into the story, to make them want to read the thing in the first place."

The chief editors and the copy desk (who write the majority of headlines) have always kept this in mind. Moreover, the grind of edit-ing a daily newspaper can be wearisome; get-ting a little clever with the headlines can keep you fresh.

Ultimately, the spirit of the desk is best summed up by Copy Chief Barry Gross: "We're a brash, kick-ass tabloid, and the heads reflect that. Why not let the readers—and the headline writers—have some fun?

"Nothing gives me greater satisfaction than watching someone thumbing through *The Post* on the subway and breaking into a smile, almost on cue, when he or she turns a page and is im-mediately tickled by one of the heads. That's my silent fist-pump 'Yes!' moment."

Robert Walsh, *New York Post* Copy Desk

Special thanks to the following contributors from the *New York Post*:

Jon Blackwell
DeDe Brown
Elizabeth Bucceri
Simon Eskow
Eric Fettmann
Tiffany Hagler
Laura Harris
Patrick Kerns
Christopher Shaw
Robert Walsh

HISTORY OF THE NEW YORK POST

POST OWNERS

1801: *The Post* is founded with $10,000 invested by leading members of the Federalist Party allied with Alexander Hamilton. The shares are evenly split between the paper's editor, a 32-year-old lawyer named William Coleman, and its 25-year-old publisher, Michael Burnham, of Hartford, Conn.

1829: Following Coleman's death, poet William Cullen Bryant is brought in as editor and given an ownership share. In 1836, after Burnham's death, Bryant becomes the principal owner.

1854: Isaac Henderson, who had joined *The Post* 15 years earlier as a clerk earning $7 a week, buys a one-third interest in the paper for $17,000. He is named publisher, although the partnership is still known as William C. Bryant & Co.

1878: Parke Godwin, Bryant's son-in-law and successor, takes control of the paper following the editor's death. He owns 50 of the 100 shares; Henderson owns 49.

1881: Hearing rumors that Henderson is preparing to sell his shares to legendary robber baron Jay Gould, Godwin sells control of *The Post* to railroad magnate Henry Villard, who had been a Civil War correspondent for Horace Greeley's *New York Tribune*. Villard also purchases *The Nation* magazine, which is issued as *The Post*'s weekly edition.

1918: With the paper losing circulation because of suggestions during World War I that it is sympathetic to Germany, Villard's son and heir, Oswald Garrison Villard, sells *The Post* to Thomas A. Lamont, a senior partner in the Wall Street firm of J. P. Morgan, but retains control of *The Nation*.

1922: Unable to stem mounting losses and unwilling to subsidize the paper further, Lamont sells out to a syndicate of 34 prominent businessman and political reformers headed by Edwin Gay, founding

dean of the Harvard Business School, who becomes the paper's editor. Among the new co-owners is future president Franklin D. Roosevelt.

1924: Like Villard, Gay is unable to turn the paper's fortunes around and runs out of working capital. *The Post* is sold to elderly magazine publisher Cyrus H. K. Curtis, owner of the *Saturday Evening Post* and the *Ladies Home Journal*.

1933: Following Curtis' death, his heirs are prepared to accept $1 million from rival publishers to shut *The Post* down for good. But FDR convinces his friend J. David Stern, a Philadelphia newspaper owner, to buy the paper and turn it into a liberal, pro– New Deal organ.

1939: With his Philadelphia newspapers under fierce financial challenge, Stern decides to sell *The Post*. FDR once again steps in and prevails on city councilman George Backer to persuade his wife, banking heiress Dorothy Schiff, to buy the paper. She will continue to run the paper's business end for the next 37 years.

1976: Fearing an upcoming change in federal tax law that would impose a large burden on her heirs, Mrs. Schiff unexpectedly decides to sell *The Post* to Australian-born publisher Rupert Murdoch.

1988: Congressional Democrats, led by Sens. Ted Kennedy and Ernest Hollings, quietly pass a rider to the federal budget forbidding new joint ownerships of print and broadcast properties in the same city. Murdoch, who has since purchased Channel 5, is forced to sell *The Post* to real estate developer Peter Kalikow.

1993: Kalikow is forced into personal bankruptcy and *The Post* soon follows. After a tumultuous period during which Steve Hoffenberg and Abe Hirschfeld serve as temporary managers of the paper, Murdoch makes a surprise bid for the paper—provided the FCC gives him a permanent waiver of the cross-ownership rule in New York. When the waiver is granted, he resumes control of the paper.

Abe Hirschfeld Episode

It's the only *New York Post* front page to appear without a headline or a photo. But, in many ways, it is the most eloquent Page One of all.

Any paper over 200 years old is going to have some rough patches. Perhaps roughest of all for *The Post* was in 1993, when the Abe Hirschfeld circus came to *The Post*'s South Street building.

Chaos had reigned ever since Rupert Murdoch was forced to sell the paper after Senator Ted Kennedy sneaked over midnight legislation eliminating cross-ownership with a TV station.

At that point, Send in the Clowns.

Real estate developer Peter Kalikow became first in line to acquire *The Post* from Murdoch. After complicated givebacks and cost reductions, Kalikow had his tabloid, and all was well . . . for a while.

There seems to be something about real estate moguls and newspaper publishing that makes for a bad mix. Eventually, financial setbacks forced Kalikow to sell.

In short, the job just didn't work out.

Kalikow's difficulties paved the way for Steven Hoffenberg. Hoffenberg, in turn, because of his own questionable financial health, let Hirschfeld in the door—the erratic developer's publishing experience came primarily from the construction of parking garages.

It was bad from the get-go. The 73-year-old loon's first mandate was that the paper publish his wife's poetry—on Page One.

After a good deal of legal wrangling, Hirschfeld forced Hoffenberg out. But Hoffenberg left one lasting legacy—and one to be proud of: He had installed newspaper legend Pete Hamill as editor of *The Post*.

To the staff's dismay, though, Hirschfeld then teamed up with Wilbert Tatum of the radical *Amsterdam News*, and their first move was to fire

five of *The Post*'s top editors and reporters, including Hamill. Chaos ensued. In retaliation, the staff compiled this special historic edition; every news article and editorial was an unrestrained attack on both Hirschfeld and Tatum. Capping it off was the memorable image of *Post* founder Alexander Hamilton shedding a tear. It was an idea that came to then managing editor Marc Kalech in the shower and was then executed perfectly by design editor Dennis Wickman.

In the face of this unprecedented staff rebellion, Hirschfeld and Tatum withdrew the firings. But they continued to dicker over the management of the paper—until former owner Rupert Murdoch heroically stepped in and rescued *The Post*.

Murdoch reacquired the paper (take that, Ted Kennedy), and, eventually, nut-job Hirschfeld landed in prison for conspiring to have a business associate killed. Hoffenberg went to jail for tax fraud. Sometimes things work out better than you could expect.

2 **   NEW YORK POST, TUESDAY, MARCH 16, 1993

An urgent appeal to Post readers: HELP!

To the readers of this paper from the editorial staff of the New York Post:

We need your help. Our paper — your paper — is being taken over by Abe Hirschfeld, a man we believe will destroy The Post, a part of this great city for 192 years. We believe Mr. Hirschfeld's basic ignorance of the way our business operates — and his refusal to educate himself — means The Post will permanently cease publication in

days. We take no issue with Mr. Hirschfeld's right to own a newspaper, but we feel The Post is too important — not only to us, but to all New Yorkers — to entrust it to him and his new partner, Wilbert Tatum. We believe Mr. Tatum's view of reality — as expressed by the journalism practiced in his Amsterdam News — is repugnant to most fair-thinking New Yorkers. The Post is more important than one man's vanity and another

man's bigotry. And it's more important than whether a bankrupt millionaire can legally escape his obligation to his workers and the nation. We ask for your help. We ask that you call Mr. Hirschfeld today at (212) 815-8152 and ask him to sell this paper to someone who will allow it to survive. Please call your representatives in City Hall, Albany and Washington and ask them to help us in any way they can. Please care.

IS THE POST PETER-ING OUT?

By MIKE PEARL, DON BRODERICK, MARIANNE GOLDSTEIN and LEO STANDORA

The New York Post's life-and-death drama reached Chapter 11 yesterday as Peter Kalikow sought bankruptcy protection for his troubled tabloid.

The surprise move came amid a bitter and rapidly changing legal battle over plans to sell the newspaper to real-estate mogul Abraham Hirschfeld.

Hirschfeld further deepened the crisis yesterday with the attempted helter-skelter firing of 72 employees, but most of the dismissals later were rescinded.

Court sources said Kalikow's unexpected bankruptcy action clearly seemed to be designed to keep a growing list of creditors off his back until the sale to Hirschfeld — or someone else — is completed.

The sale is being contested by debt-collection tycoon Steven Hoffenberg, who a month ago came in at the last minute to save The Post from closing, and thought he was going to be The Post's new owner.

According to sources, Kalikow fears that if his deal with Hirschfeld falls through or stalls, anxious creditors — including Uncle Sam — will begin suing him for what's due them.

Kalikow's lawyers showed up in Bankruptcy Court yesterday to file the papers at 8:55 a.m. His legal crew used the same get-there-early and strike-first strategy to save their boss' financial skin two years ago, when Kalikow filed for personal bankruptcy protection.

In the intervening years, Kalikow has maintained a lavish lifestyle of luxury cars, opulent homes, yachts and expensive parties — while The Post was financially hemorrhaging.

He even had the audacity to wage a costly legal battle with East Hampton zoning officials to build a special dock alongside his vast Mon-

ABE, WILBERT AND THE POST: EDITORIAL / P. 24

tauk estate to provide parking for his extra-large yacht.

Kalikow apparently continued to take care of No.1 as the current crisis began taking shape in late 1992.

Although $4.5 million in FICA payments was withheld from Post employees' paychecks, he never turned that money over to the federal government.

If he doesn't ante up soon, he could be prosecuted.

He apparently was so strapped for money he also withheld $30,000 in payments to the 401K retirement accounts of his New York Newspaper Guild's employees, but never passed the funds on to the mutual-fund company.

The Manhattan district attorney is poised to investigate if he doesn't pay up soon.

In addition, creditors ranging from ink and paper suppliers to elevator repairmen and messenger services all report Kalikow has stiffed them for hundreds of thousands.

Kalikow also has reneged on his promise to give the unions a 20 percent stake in the paper — in exchange for their 20 percent paycut.

He has mortgaged The Post's headquarters at 210

South St. — the paper's single asset, its underpinning for future operations and the sole source of funds to cover the employees' severance liability for retirees and other staffers in the event of a shutdown.

The continuing chaos at The Post kept the newspaper from publishing Monday's editions — the first time the newspaper has failed to reach the newsstands since a citywide newspaper strike in 1978.

Contributing greatly to the confusion was Hirschfeld's announcement Sunday night that he planned to fire 270 randomly chosen employees.

The "hit list" supposedly was drawn up by Hirschfeld and the man he said is his new partner — Amsterdam News publisher Wilbert Tatum.

Hirschfeld, who changes his mind as quickly and as often as a traffic light blinks, yesterday told the Associated Press that if Gov. Cuomo comes forward with a new group of investors, he would consider stepping out of the picture.

"The best thing I would like is to buy the building, not The Post," said Hirschfeld, 74, admitting, "I don't know anything about newspapers."

Cuomo, at a news conference yesterday, said he and state Economic Development Commissioner Vincent Tese were getting calls from people interested in helping.

He would not reveal any names.

"The bottom line is we're trying to keep the paper alive," Cuomo said.

"It is kind of zany at the moment," the governor had said earlier in the day. "But it can be righted. We can get an established owner, whether it's Mr. Hirschfeld or someone else."

Although most union members fired yesterday were rehired, the fate of 20 managers and non-union employees who were canned remained unclear last night.

Part of the ongoing battle over The Post was fought in State Supreme Court yesterday, where Hoffenberg sought a temporary restraining order to stop the sale to Hirschfeld.

At the hearing, Justice Stanley Sklar told lawyers for Hoffenberg that he could not overrule the federal order giving Hirschfeld the right to assume ownership from Kalikow.

Ed Wallace, one of Hoffenberg's lawyers, told the court his client had been betrayed by the man he brought in as

"his partner."

At the hearing, the paper's vice president and comptroller, Stephen Bumbaca, testified that The Post had run out of funds and told reporters he needs $1.5 million immediately to keep the paper operating this week.

"I need it now," Bumbaca said.

The legal action later switched to Bankruptcy Court, where a judge set a hearing on a raft of motions for Friday.

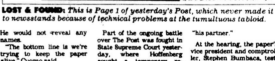

NEW YORK POST
SPORTS EXTRA

MONDAY, MARCH 15, 1993

Post staff to Abe Hirschfeld . . .
GET LOST!
Reporters, editors outraged over planned layoffs

Real estate developer Abe Hirschfeld yesterday was assailed by Post reporters and editors after he ordered a "hit" list of 270 workers. He also denied firing Post editor Pete Hamill but the newspaper's executives called Hirschfeld a liar.

LOST & FOUND: This is Page 1 of yesterday's Post, which never made it to newsstands because of technical problems at the tumultuous tabloid.

INDEX	Social Security Sweepstakes: Page 26			WEATHER	LOTTERY	The Post uses recycled paper

WEATHER
TODAY: Sunny. High 40 to 45.
TONIGHT: Cloudy, chance of rain. Low in the upper 30s.
TOMORROW: Cloudy, rain likely. High 45 to 50.
EXTENDED OUTLOOK: Sunny Thursday and Friday; chance of snow Saturday. Highs in the 30s, lows in the teens to the 20s.
SUNSET: 6:04 **SUNRISE TOM'W:** 6:05

LOTTERY

76 Volume 192, Number 101 Copyright 1993, The New York Post Company Inc. Published daily except Sundays and certain holidays by the New York Post Company, Inc., 210 South Street, New York, N.Y. 10002-7807. Second-class postage paid at New York, N.Y. (USPS 383-200). Main office phone: 212-815-8000. News tips: 212-815-8500. Classified advertising: 212-815-8100. Retail advertising: 212-815-8437. Mail subscription information: All orders, changes of address and inquiries, contact Kingston Newspaper Mailing Co., P.O. Box 1517, Kingston, N.Y. 12401, or phone 1-800-724-0661. Foreign and domestic mail subscription rates available upon request to the Kingston Newspaper Mailing Co. For home delivery, phone 1-800-552-POST.

NEW YORK POST, TUESDAY, MARCH 16, 1993 ★★ 3

WHO IS THIS NUT?

YECHHH! *Miami Herald reporter Bonnie Weston turns away in disgust after finding herself a-wearin' of the green — in the form of a slimy hock of Abe Hirschfeld's opinion of her coverage of his political campaigns and his ownership of the Clarion Castle Hotel.*

Post isn't only hostage Abe's taken

By COLIN MINER

Real-estate mogul and Post owner-wannabe Abe Hirschfeld prides himself on being spontaneous, on not getting bogged down by planning too far ahead.

It's just that quality, he recently told a reporter, that led him to get involved with the New York Post.

That quality also has immersed him in perhaps the biggest controversy of his career.

"The entire staff does not want him here," one editor said.

"Maybe on this occasion, he should have thought ahead."

What has The Post staff concerned is Hirschfeld's apparent instability.

"Hanging out with Abe Hirschfeld is like inhaling secondhand smoke from an opium pipe," wrote Molly Gordy in a 1992 Newsday profile. "Hour by hour, it gets harder and harder to distinguish reality from fantasy."

The 73-year old developer, who made his money in parking garages and health clubs, bought his first building in 1954 and was embroiled in tenant problems and building-code violations when he resold it a couple of years later.

It was Hirschfeld's parking-garage interests that first gave him a special place in the annals of New York City.

In 1976, he went into the office of Dorothy Green, head of the city's environmental-impact division, and announced he was holding her hostage until she approved a clean-air permit for one of his garages.

She was eventually rescued by officials who broke down a door. She later filed suit against Hirschfeld and settled out of court for approximately $35,000.

Another Hirschfeld controversy involved Lincoln West, the massive development he proposed for Manhattan's Penn Yards — now the site of Donald Trump's proposed Riverside South, of which Hirschfeld owns 20 percent.

That controversy involved a 1982 meeting between Hirschfeld and Sen. Alfonse D'Amato, which resulted in D'Amato pledging his support for the Lincoln West proposal.

News reports later alleged that the meeting had been set up as the result of a $10,000 payment to a Long Island lawyer friendly with both D'Amato and Hirschfeld.

While all parties denied wrongdoing, it was never disputed that Hirschfeld's partners paid the lawyer.

Hirschfeld has been described as vengeful by those who have been

See NUT *on Page 18*

Part of her job was taking a gob from angry slob

Bonnie Weston's 15 minutes of fame came when Abe Hirschfeld spit on her and a Miami television news crew caught it on tape.

Weston, a reporter for the Miami Herald, was covering the auction of a Hirschfeld property when Hirschfeld let the spittle fly.

His reason: Weston had been responsible for most of the Herald's coverage of "Honest Abe," as he likes to call himself.

Hirschfeld had a stormy relationship with Miami Beach, where Weston is based. From May 1990, when she arrived at the Herald, through Hirschfeld's stay in Miami Beach, Weston covered the carpetbagger from New York — from his controversial ownership of the Clarion Castle Hotel through his unsuccessful run for mayor.

Weston covered all his foibles and follies, and Hirschfeld was not appreciative.

She was there in October 1990, when Hirschfeld found it necessary to auction off one of his money-losing properties. And that's when he felt there was only one way he could properly express his feelings about her coverage.

By spitting on her.

Weston did not wish to discuss the incident yesterday. She said lawyers for the Herald had asked her not to comment because of a pending lawsuit filed by Hirschfeld in January against her newspaper.

Still, Weston continues to cover Abe's Miami operations. People at the newspaper said yesterday that its coverage of Hirschfeld has not been affected by the incident, and Weston continues to cover him.

Colin Miner

It's adios ads if Terrible Two take over

By CHARLES CARILLO

The Post can say goodbye to about a quarter of a million dollars worth of ads right off the bat, if Abe Hirschfeld stays at the helm of the newspaper.

Two significant clients in particular made it clear that if things stay as they are, they'll pull their ads. Both requested to remain anonymous.

"We don't want any part of the paper if the scenario remains the same," a client worth about $200,000 per year told The Post.

A second client, worth about $50,000, vowed: "If Mr. [Bill] Tatum is controlling this place, we're out

of here, because he's a racist."

Tatum, publisher of the Amsterdam News, was named by Hirschfeld as the Post's co-publisher and a managing editor. He is perhaps best known for his decision to print the identity of the Central Park jogger who was raped and assaulted by a gang of youths.

Tatum also supported Tawana Brawley in the face of a grand-jury conclusion that she fabricated a story that she was abducted and raped by cops.

"Clients have been calling all morning," a Post employee, who spoke on the condition of anonymity, said yesterday.

"They want to know what's happening, and whether we're going to publish or not.

"I told them to sit tight, that we're not sure what the whole scenario's going to be, and not to make any hasty decisions.

"They said they would. These people are going to sit tight. I told them, 'The hand is not played out yet.'"

Callers who placed classified ads were calling to pull them from the paper because "they said [Hirschfeld and Tatum] are crazy . . . They definitely think [Hirschfeld is] nuts," said the Post employee.

Display- and classified-advertis-

ing clients were not the only ones calling The Post for updates on whether the paper would continue to publish and whether advertising was being accepted.

"Hey, we love you," one would-be advertiser said. "But these guys who are coming in to take it over . . . I don't know whether I could stay with you."

Out of the hundreds of calls received by the Post city desk, not one call was in support of Hirschfeld and Tatum.

"I am a black American and I'm against Hirschfeld and Tatum because they pander to the radical fringe," said David

White, a Post reader.

A woman who is a history teacher in the New York City school system said, "It's totally outrageous that Tatum is going to be the editor of The Post. He already has a voice in the Amsterdam News. He is a racist. He printed the name of the jogger during the [Central Park] trial when no other paper did. It's just outrageous."

A male caller said: "As long as Hirschfeld and Tatum are running The Post, I will never buy it again. And I know many other loyal Post readers who feel the same way."

NEW YORK POST, TUESDAY, MARCH 16, 1993

5

HATE-'EM TATUM READY FOR SLIME TIME

By MEL JUFFE

Bill Tatum, the man just named editor of the New York Post by Abe Hirschfeld, brings a controversial journalistic record to his new job.

As chief editor of the Amsterdam News, Wilbert Tatum vigorously supported the likes of Tawana Brawley, Prof. Leonard Jeffries and the youths who were convicted of rape in the Central Park jogger case. He also opened his paper's pages to virulent anti-Semitic comment.

Mayor Koch, saying he detected "rank racism" in the Amsterdam News, once said Tatum was "guilty of polarizing this town."

Pete Hamill, the Post editor fired by Hirschfeld to make way for Tatum, said:

"Under Tatum, the Amsterdam News has published more anti-Semitic drivel than anything since [the Nazi newspaper] *Der Stuermer.* The man has no daily-newspaper experience and has never explained his blind support of the Tawana Brawley hoax.

"Instead of using his paper to calm people's emotions and to remove hatreds, he fed it — by supporting the Brawley hoax and the guys who raped the jogger in Central Park."

In a report last June, the Anti-Defamation League said the Amsterdam News was "the most provocative" of the three black newspapers in the city that evidence a pattern of hostility toward Jews.

The paper's "tone and content often have an emotional, even incendiary, quality, largely representing the point of view of its editor, Wilbert Tatum," the report said.

Tatum, the report went on, "was regarded by the Jewish community as someone with whom dialogue could be conducted, and he encouraged that notion. In the Crown Heights crisis, however, Tatum emerged as an influential figure willing to inflame community passions."

At the jogger trial three years ago, Tatum showed up at the court house to make a public display of his support for the defendants.

He stood proudly with the defendants' supporters as they chanted: "The boyfriend did it!" He tried to stop a Post photographer from taking the picture of the mother of one defendant.

Tatum even provided transportation for the defendants' backers to the courthouse, according to reporters at the scene.

But what really shocked the city was Tatum's decision to publish the name of the gang-rape victim — while other

See TATUM *on Page 17*

LIP SERVICE: *Salivating Abe Hirschfeld plants a big, slurpy, sloppy wet one on his editor-appointee, Wilbert Tatum, at a Post press conference.*

New York Post: Robin Graubard

Assemblyman: We'll boycott Post if Wild Bill is the editor

A PROMINENT Jewish lawmaker yesterday vowed to lead a "citywide boycott" of the New York Post if Amsterdam News publisher Wilbert Tatum becomes the new editor-in-chief.

Democratic state Assemblyman Dov Hikind, an influential Orthodox Jew from Borough Park, said he would lead the boycott because Tatum has fomented "anti-Jewish and anti-Israel hysterics" on the pages of his black-oriented newspaper.

Meanwhile, other lawmakers here also warned that The Post would, in the words of one, "lose all credibility" if erratic millionaire Abe Hirschfeld was allowed to remain as the paper's owner.

"Bill Tatum's newspaper, with its racially inflammatory articles, shares the blame for the [1991] Crown Heights riots," said Hikind.

"The thought of Tatum now becoming editor of The Post should be terrifying to all New Yorkers and especially Jewish New Yorkers because he has re-

FREDRIC DICKER
INSIDE ALBANY

peatedly published viciously anti-Semitic articles," said Hikind.

The assemblyman said it was especially "outrageous" that Tatum's newspaper repeatedly printed highly slanted articles backing the anti-Semitic and anti-white rantings and racial theories of disgraced City College Professor Leonard Jeffries. Both Gov. Cuomo and Mayor Dinkins strongly denounced Jeffries' remarks as racially divisive.

Hikind, meanwhile, said it was

"shocking" that current Post boss Hirschfeld, who is Jewish, had hired Tatum.

"It's one thing to laugh at Hirschfeld, which I think a lot of people have been doing for a long time. It's another thing to have him do something this damaging," said Hikind.

"The Jewish community will boycott The Post with Tatum there and I and many others will lead the boycott," said Hikind, an increasingly influential politician who is eying a race for city

See DICKER *on Page 21*

6

NEW YORK POST, TUESDAY, MARCH 16, 1993

Abe Hirschfeld's sick jokes

By FRANK DiGIACOMO,
FLORENCE ANTHONY
and TIMOTHY McDARRAH

Dial B for Bill

Back in August 1990, when **Bill Tatum** ran the name of the Central Park jogger rape victim in his Amsterdam News, most of the media was outraged. But Screw publisher **Al Goldstein** took matters into his own hands. As we reported then, Goldstein ran Tatum's home address and phone number in his paper and repeated it on his late night cable sex show, "Midnight Blue." "He wants equal treatment of blacks and whites," Goldstein said of the controversial Tatum. "Well, here it is." Responded Tatum that week: "Bleep him. I'll run his mama's name and address in my paper next week." One problem: Goldstein's mom had been dead for years.

Koch vs Tatum

July 12, 1984. Mayor **Ed Koch** and Amsterdam News editor **Bill Tatum**, in a bitter radio debate, last night accused each other of polarizing the city racially. In the shouting match, Tatum accused Koch of "exacerbating the schism between blacks and whites." Koch, defending his refusal to use racial quotas, shot back that Tatum was being typically "outrageous and unfair."

MASON: the name game.
WE don't know what **Jackie Mason** thinks of Abe **Hirschfeld** these days. We are certain that back in 1989 the comedian had a very low opinion of the real-estate developer. These are just some of the names that Mason called Hirschfeld at a deposition, according to a 1989 Post story. That's the time when the two bigshots were suing each other over Abe's claims that he had gotten Jackie's career on track. Before Mason's attorney, **Raoul Felder**, could muzzle his client, Jackie said of Hirschfeld: "...you phony bastard.. You are a sick liar... You bleeping pig. You are a common deranged maniac. .You should drop dead by Thursday...."

IF Wilbert Tatum does end up working with **Abe Hirschfeld**, the Amsterdam News publisher should refrain from asking his purported partner if he's heard any good jokes.

Back in Jan. 14, 1991, PAGE SIX reported that some racially charged comments by Hirschfeld had Miami Beach City Commissioners wondering if the real estate developer and former New York office seeker has a vacancy problem — between his ears.

Hirschfeld had city planners gunning for his resignation from the commission - to which he was elected in 1989 - after he told two off-color ethnic gags and accused another city commissioner of public drunkenness.

The Miami Beach brouhaha began on Dec. 19, 1990 when, shortly before a commission meeting, Hirschfeld decided to entertain the waiting citizens with an ethnic joke that involved blacks and Jews.

According to minutes of the meeting obtained by PAGE SIX, the brassy builder persisted in telling the yarn despite the protests of Miami Beach Mayor **Alex Daoud**, who apparently already had heard the off-color story.

"Abe was the only who laughed," said one source who witnessed the event. "Everyone else looked astounded."

On Dec. 26, 1990, Commissioner **William Shockett** called an emergency meeting to demand Hirschfeld's resignation. Instead, Hirschfeld retold the joke to an incredulous crowd, substituting Arabs for blacks.

That same evening, a local Miami television station aired Abe's comment that Shockett often came to commission meetings "drunk."

Shockett sued Hirschfeld for slander but dropped the complaint when Hirschfeld issued a formal letter of apology.

Shortly after Hirschfeld's repeat performance, the commissioners decided against seeking Abe's resignation, because, said Commissioner **Martin Shapiro**:"It's obvious Commissioner Hirschfeld is not a man who can be embarrassed or humiliated."

Hirschfeld, at the time, said he "was just trying to entertain the people in the room prior to the meeting."

Hirschfeld said that he retold the joke to point out that it "came from a book, 'The Last Official Jewish Joke Book.' What's wrong with that?"

"I'm extremely happy that I told the joke," admitted Abe. "I never would have gotten the publicity that I'm getting if I hadn't told it."

ABE HIRSCHFELD MANAGES THE POST WITH THE STYLE AND DIGNITY THAT'S BECOME HIS TRADEMARK OVER THE YEARS

Pay up, Abe

IF multimillionaire Abe Hirschfeld wants to know why he's always losing, perhaps it's because he doesn't know how to act like a champ. Hirschfeld is refusing to pay from 50 to 60 New Yorkers — many of them unemployed — who were hired to pass out his congressional campaign literature outside polling places on primary day during his failed Congressional seat bid. Back then, the developer claimed at first that "everyone has been paid." But after we'd talked to more than six who say they're each owed $112.50 for 15 hours of work, and called Hirschfeld back, he said: "I told [coordinator] **Tom Bartosiewicz** to hire a maximum of 18 people, and he hired 65 people." Says one man: "I started at 6 in the morning and worked until 9 o'clock at night. I'm not trying to cause trouble for anybody, but it's wrong."

Also-ran Abe loses another one

THE jury punished **Abe Hirschfeld** for unfairly evicting a restaurateur in his Castle Hotel in Miami, but it could do nothing about his singing. Back in the summer of 1991, the parking lot mogul was being sued for $1.2 million by restaurateur **Leila Hunter**, owner of Blackie's in his Castle Hotel in Miami. Hunter claimed that on the day after Christmas and without warning, Hirschfeld had sent 11 men to escort her from her restaurant, forcing her to leave everything — including the money in the register — behind. After lawyer **Howard Talenfeld** reportedly "took Hirschfeld apart on the stand," the jury came back in 20 minutes awarding Hunter double what she'd asked for. "It shows that no matter how much money you have, it's not cool to go above the law," Hunter told PAGE SIX then. "What happened was, we had to put up a temporary wall and were only using half the space we rented. All of a sudden one day we heard things on the other side of the wall. He had moved a competitor — **Sharon Bagel** — into my space." Worse, Hirschfeld "reopened the restaurant two days" after her eviction, Hunter says. "He started using my food and my equipment. It was rather ludicrous." But not as ludicrous as his TV performance after the verdict. The developer, who somehow won election to the Miami City Council after losing bids for the Senate, City Council, and lieutenant governor in New York, announced his campaign for mayor of Miami. When a Miami Herald reporter asked about the restaurant case, Hirschfeld said he hadn't lost "a minute's sleep," put on a hard hat and broke into "The Star Spangled Banner."

Block that pix

WHILE his Amsterdam News was printing the Central Park Jogger rape victim's name, publisher **Bill Tatum** was running interference for one of the defendant's mothers. Back in July 1990, The Post reported that Tatum — his press credentials dangling from his neck — tried to block Post photographer **Paul Adao**, who was snapping a picture of **Cheroney Salaam**, the mother of Central Park jogger rape case defendant **Yusef Salaam**, as she left the courthouse. Tatum, a supporter of the defendants, later denied that he had tried to interfere with Adao's newsgathering.

SMITH: rape case.
In addition to naming the Central Park jogger, **Bill Tatum** also named the victim in the Willie Smith rape case down in Palm Beach before she went public. The first one to attack him was **Lisa Sliwa**, the Guardian Angel-turned-morning radio host on WABC with hubby **Curtis**. When, as we reported, she asked Tatum on the air last April why he printed **Patricia Bowman**'s name, Tatum replied: "that's between you white folks." When Sliwa pointed out that Tatum's wife, **Susan**, is white, the portly publisher said he didn't want to talk any longer and hung up.

GENERAL NEWS

Taken kickin' and screamin'

An angry Juan Emilio Robles tries to kick a photographer yesterday as detectives took him in to be booked for the murder last year of Chase Manhattan exec Kathleen Williams. Robles, a hulking 20-year-old ex-con, is accused of stabbing the 30-year-old victim during a bungled robbery attempt on a stairway at the Waldorf-Astoria Hotel in midtown. Story on Page 14.

Headless Body in Topless Bar

It's been ridiculed and vilified, celebrated and imitated. It inspired an otherwise forgettable 1995 movie of the same name. In 2003 *New York Magazine* named it *The Post*'s single greatest headline of the past 35 years. Has there ever been a more memorable front-page headline than "Headless Body in Topless Bar"?

And the most amazing thing about the headline—written by V. A. Musetto—is that it describes the story perfectly and succinctly.

A gunman had robbed a Bronx strip club and forced all the customers and employees into a back room—where he killed, and then decapitated, one of them.

As legendary *Post* editor and columnist Steve Dunleavy later recalled: "How do you tell a sensational story other than sensationally? What should it say: 'Decapitated cerebellum in licensed premises, wherein ladies baring mammaries have been seen, to wit, performing acts counter to social mores'? I don't think so."

COP SLAIN ON EVE OF SANDS' FUNERAL PAGE NINE

TODAY

TONIGHT

TOMORROW

Details, Page 1

NEW YORK POST

METRO
TODAY'S RACING

TV listings: P. 67

THURSDAY, MAY 7, 1981

25 CENTS

© 1981 News Group Publications Inc Vol. 180, No. 167

AMERICA'S FASTEST-GROWING NEWSPAPER

AVERAGE DAILY SALES SECOND **730,000**

PHANTOM OF OPERA'S BIZARRE CONFESSION:

'She was nice to me, then I kicked her off the roof'

FULL STORY: PAGE THREE

'SNOOPY' SPY JET IN DEATH PLUNGE

Pentagon experts sift the wreckage of a missile-tracking plane that exploded in midair and crashed 43 miles west of Baltimore, Md., yesterday killing all 21 people on board. "Plane just de blew up in midair," said an Air Force spokesman as an immediate investigation was launched into the possibility of sabotage. The plane, an EC-135 (inset) is super secret, snoopy-nosed aircraft used for tracking missiles. Details: Page 2.

Top cop Ward admits jail trysts PAGE SEVEN

TONIGHT: Partly cloudy, mid 50s
TOMORROW: Increasing cloudiness, low 70s
Details, Page 2

NEW YORK POST

FINAL
WALL STREET EXTRA

TV listings: P. 91 THURSDAY, OCTOBER 18, 1984 **30** CENTS AMERICA'S FASTEST-GROWING NEWSPAPER © 1984 News Group Publications Inc. Vol. 183, No. 290 ABC AVERAGE SALES EXCEED **960,000**

400 COPS RAID TERROR GANG

NINE PALS OF BRINK'S MOB SEIZED: PAGE 13

'Million $ madam':
Her family came over
on the Mayflower

EXCLUSIVE
Post photos
and story

Alleged madam Sydney Barrows, charged as Sheila Devin, frolics on a European beach in photo taken on summer vacation. The Post learned today that she is a Mayflower descendant and blueblood belonging to one of the oldest families in America.

Exclusive photo by Steve Rosenberg

HOTEL FIREBUG KILLS 13 AND HURTS 60 Pages 4 and 5

Mayflower Madam

It was a great story, even without the kicker *The Post* eventually uncovered.

Sheila Devin, a glamorous 32-year-old blonde, had been arrested on charges of running a high-price prostitution service. Her girls collected $400 an hour and $2,000 for all-night trysts with some of Manhattan's major movers and shakers. Indeed, the prostitutes showed up to their assignments carrying briefcases with portable credit-card machines.

At first, all anyone was concerned about was Devin's little black book of clients. Were there any big names in it—and would they be made public? Police sources tantalized the press with reports of high-profile executives, politicians, Arab sheiks, movie stars, and prominent society figures.

One cop said the list read like *Who's Who*. Turns out he was pretty close.

But *The Post* received a tip that Sheila Devin was an even bigger blueblood than some of her clients—that, in fact, she was a member of the prestigious Biddle family, which traced its roots to the Pilgrims who came over on the *Mayflower* and whose members were listed in the Social Register.

Post reporter Peter Fearon managed to get her alone following her next court appearance. "We know you're a Biddle," he said. Her wide-eyed gasp was all the confirmation the paper needed. Devin's real name, it turned out, was Sidney Biddle Barrows—and her Social Register listing made the next day's *Post* headline inevitable: The paper was the first to dub her the notorious Mayflower Madam.

TODAY
Partly sunny, mid 80s
TONIGHT
Mostly clear, 65-70
TOMORROW
Partly sunny, 80-85
Details, Page 2

NEW YORK POST

METRO
TODAY'S RACING

TV listings: P. 75

TUESDAY   JULY 30   1985   **35** CENTS   ★   © 1985 News Group Publications Inc.   Vol. 184, No. 217
40 cents beyond 50-mile zone, except L.I.   **AMERICA'S FASTEST-GROWING NEWSPAPER**

ABC AVERAGE
SALES EXCEED   **900,000**

EATEN ALIVE!

Giant tigers kill pretty zoo keeper who 'loved all animals'

TRAGIC PHOTOS: PAGE 3

$1.1 BILLION ROCKEFELLER CENTER DEAL

See **BUSINESS TUESDAY** — Page 29

24-year-old Bronx Zoo keeper Robin Silverman who was mauled to death yesterday.

FOUNDED IN 1801 BY ALEXANDER HAMILTON

NEW YORK POST

SPORTS FINAL

THURSDAY, APRIL 21, 1988 / Clouds, chance of showers, clearing, 60 today; clear, cool, 40 tonight / Details, Page 2

35¢ in New York City   50¢ elsewhere

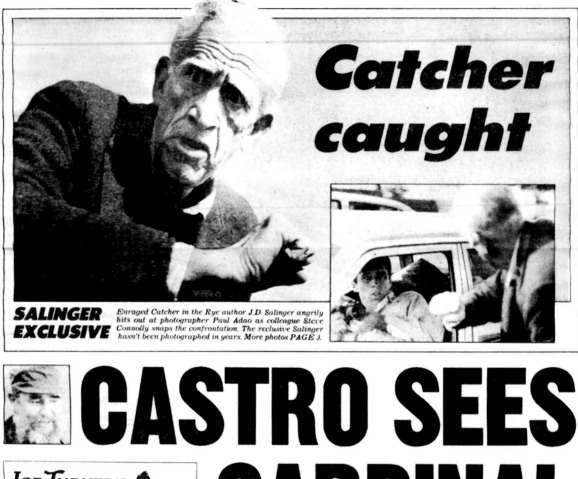

Catcher caught

SALINGER EXCLUSIVE

Enraged Catcher in the Rye author J.D. Salinger angrily hits out at photographer Paul Adao as colleague Steve Connolly snaps the confrontation. The reclusive Salinger hasn't been photographed in years. More photos PAGE 3.

CASTRO SEES CARDINAL

JOE TURNER'S COME AND GONE

AUGUST WILSON Portrait of a great writer
Page 33

By JERRY NACHMAN

HAVANA — Fidel Castro had a historic meeting with John Cardinal O'Connor last night — but in a fit of presidential pique the Cuban leader decided to deny the world an opportunity to see them together.

Castro, through a Foreign Ministry representative, said he would not let the press photograph or witness the meeting between the two

Continued on Page 2

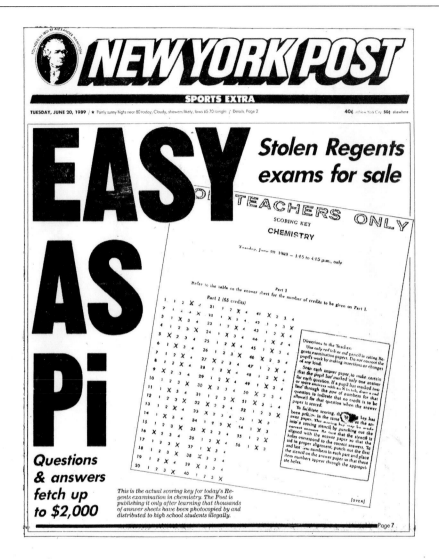

Easy as Pi

Post editor Jerry Nachman was intrigued when one of his reporters, who worked as an adviser to several high school newspapers, told him that the answers to the next day's New York State Regents exam in chemistry—a major factor in both grades and college admissions for 80,000 students—were widely available on a thriving black market. To prove his point, the reporter made a phone call—and just 10 minutes later the answer key was rolling off the city room fax machine.

Nachman's immediate response: "Let's publish the answers on Page One." Embarrassed education officials were forced to cancel the exam. And they lashed out at *The Post*, calling its decision to publish "beneath contempt" and threatening to sue.

But it took an editorial in the *New York Times*, of all places, to put "Easy as Pi" into perspective: What really happened, the paper said, was that "a mischievous newspaper did its job—it exposed a cheating scandal." Officials would do better, the editorial added, "to listen to the message and remedy the problem." Which is exactly what they did—thanks to a little prodding from *The Post*.

NEW YORK POST

LATE CITY FINAL

WEDNESDAY, OCTOBER 25, 1989 / ★★ R Sunny, 70s today, clear, mid 40s tonight / Details Page 2

40¢ in New York City 50¢ elsewhere

JUDGMENT DAY

Rev. Jim Bakker gets 45 years . . .

but for Zsa Zsa — only three days

ZSA ZSA GABOR
12G in fines too.

Rev. Jim Bakker is led away in handcuffs after sentencing yesterday.

UPI Photo

A TALE OF TWO JAILBIRDS: PAGE THREE

Dead German shepherd is covered by ASPCA foreman Phil Zachman at their headquarters on 92nd Street yesterday.

Run Down Like a Dog

If there's one thing *Post* editors have learned over the years, it's that nothing tears at readers' heartstrings like an animal story. And few *Post* stories have created the level of public outcry as the heartrending saga of Token, the German Shepherd that was run down by a subway train.

It was outraged riders themselves who alerted the paper to what had happened. A southbound D train was stopped for 20 minutes as cops searched for a dog that had been seen on the tracks. When they couldn't find him, the car was ordered to move—moments later, said one rider, "we heard the most horrible, blood-curdling scream." The dog, badly wounded, was euthanized shortly after.

Reporter Bill Hoffmann, ordered by Metro editor John Cotter to "name that dog," came up with Token as he fielded angry calls from passengers demanding that someone pay a price for what had happened. The ASPCA filed formal charges against the subway motorman who'd ordered the train forward—even as Transit Authority officials defended him as a dog owner himself.

Two days later, the motorman agreed to speak publicly—as long as he wasn't identified. "I'm not a killer," he pleaded. "I couldn't sleep for two days knowing that I hurt this animal. There was real eye contact between me and the dog."

Eventually, the furor subsided and no one faced charges. But *Post* readers didn't forget Token: When the ASPCA offered to place a plaque on its building to memorialize the slain pooch, readers responded with $10,000 in donations. And, sure enough, the plaque went up—where it remains today.

NEW YORK POST

LATE CITY FINAL

SATURDAY, JUNE 22/SUNDAY, JUNE 23, 1991   ★ ★   Partly sunny, high 80s today; partly cloudy, low 60s tonight   ::   Details, Page 2

40¢ in New York City 50¢ elsewhere

NO NUDES IS GOOD NUDES

– high court rules 5-4

The HOME of... Topless Dancers DAILY & NIGHTLY

Sign like this outside Queens tavern may become a thing of the past.

Flash Dancers

Yesterday's Supreme Court ruling means local community groups can now push for laws to ban topless joints like this one in Midtown.

Community leaders moving for topless ban here –Page 5

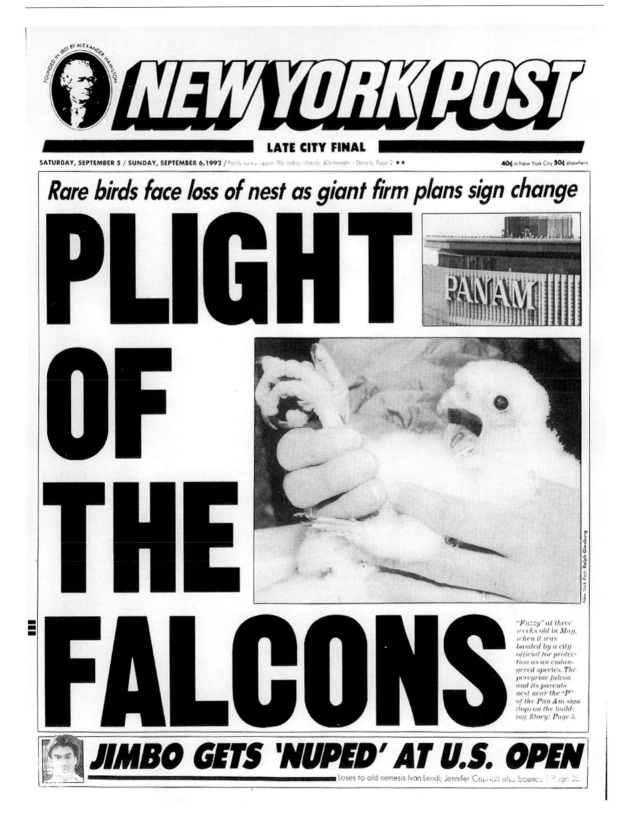

FOUNDED IN 1801 BY ALEXANDER HAMILTON

NEW YORK POST

LATE CITY FINAL

SATURDAY, SEPTEMBER 5 / SUNDAY, SEPTEMBER 6, 1992 / Partly sunny, upper 70s today; cloudy, 60s tonight / Details, Page 2 ★★

40¢ in New York City 50¢ elsewhere

Rare birds face loss of nest as giant firm plans sign change

PLIGHT OF THE FALCONS

"Fuzzy" at three weeks old in May, when it was banded by a city official for protection as an endangered species. The peregrine falcon and its parents nest near the "P" of the Pan Am sign (top on the building). Story: Page 5.

New York Post: Ralph Ginzburg

JIMBO GETS 'NUPED' AT U.S. OPEN

Loses to old nemesis Ivan Lendl; Jennifer Capriati also bounced / Page 32

See page 2

See page 3

See page 7

ASSAD'S SON IS KILLED IN CAR CRASH

PLUCKY POOCH TAKES THE LONG WAY HOME

RUDY FINDS IT TOUGH TO FILL TOP JOBS

FOUNDED IN 1801 BY ALEXANDER HAMILTON

NEW YORK POST

METRO EDITION

SATURDAY, JANUARY 22 / SUNDAY, JANUARY 23, 1994 / High 30 today; sun tomorrow / Details, Page 10   50¢

LORENA CUT LOOSE

Full story: Pages 4 & 5

Not guilty due to temporary insanity

Lorena Bobbitt will go free after a jury decided she was temporarily insane when she cut off her husband's penis with a kitchen knife.

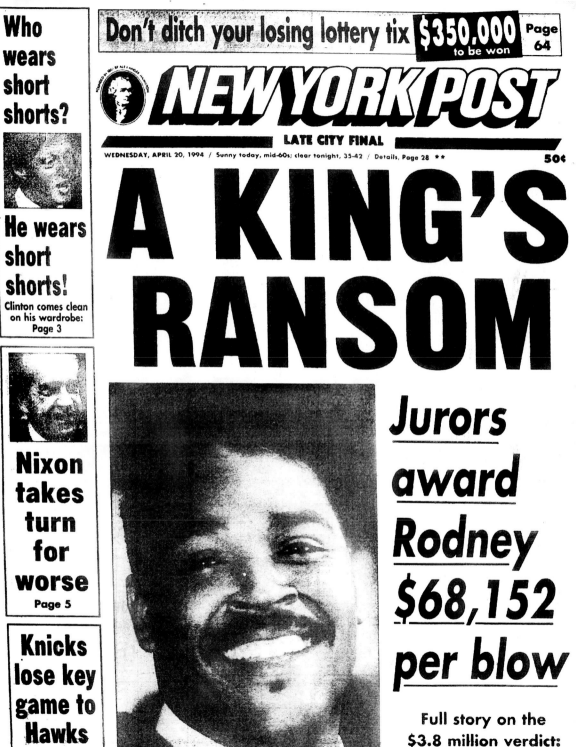

Who wears short shorts?

He wears short shorts!
Clinton comes clean on his wardrobe:
Page 3

Nixon takes turn for worse
Page 5

Knicks lose key game to Hawks
Pages 74-75

Don't ditch your losing lottery tix $350,000 to be won
Page 64

NEW YORK POST

LATE CITY FINAL

WEDNESDAY, APRIL 20, 1994 / Sunny today, mid-60s; clear tonight, 35-42 / Details, Page 28 ★★ 50¢

A KING'S RANSOM

Jurors award Rodney $68,152 per blow

Full story on the $3.8 million verdict:
Page 4

Rodney King, whose videotaped beating by cops sparked the worst riot in modern U.S. history, originally sought $15 million in his suit against L.A.

ValuJet on brink after FAA grounding
Page 7

Filegate aide is put on leave
Page 2

Police eye more victims of Royster
Pages 4 & 5

NEW YORK POST

HOME DELIVERY
1-800-940-7678
CALL TODAY!

LATE CITY FINAL

TUESDAY, JUNE 18, 1996 / Showers possible today, upper 70s; cloudy tonight, mid 60s / Details, Page 82 ★★

·· 50¢

Cops throw feisty widow, 86, in jail after minor traffic mishap

GRANNY IN THE SLAMMER

New York Post: Michael Alexander

Ruth Michel endured a 23-hour nightmare at Central Booking in the city jail after she was arrested by half a dozen policemen. Some, she says, had drawn guns.

EXCLUSIVE:
See Page 3

Cleanup begins after twisters claim 24

PAGE 12

Furor as school guard admits he's a Latin King

PAGE 3

NEW YORK POST

METRO EDITION

MONDAY, MARCH 3, 1997 / Afternoon rain, 38–43 / Weather: Page 22

http://www.nypostonline.com/ · · · 50¢

Giuliani in wig and gown

Rudy the cutie

PAGE 6

Bill's big bucks donors go into hiding

PAGE 2

O'C, pope: Don't monkey with man

SIN IN THE CLONES

FULL STORY: PAGES 4 & 5

Just as it was being revealed that researchers in Oregon had produced these cloned monkeys, Cardinal O'Connor joined Pope John Paul yesterday in condemning human cloning experiments.

Associated Press

NEW YORK POST

HOME DELIVERY
1-800-940-7678
CALL TODAY!

LATE CITY FINAL

FRIDAY, MARCH 28, 1997 / Sunny, 60 / Weather: Page 42 ★ ★   http://www.nypostonline.com/   · · · 50¢

'FOLLOW ME'

Marshall Applewhite, a.k.a. Do, the leader of the bizarre cyber-cult shown in a videotape produced shortly before the group's mass suicide.

Why suicide cult followed mental patient to 'spaceship'

COMPLETE MASS SUICIDE COVERAGE STARTS ON PAGE 2

Charles Kuralt dead at 62

PAGE 2

Kuralt

Yanks swap Duncan, Rogers for Vaughn

PAGE 46

NEW YORK POST

HOME DELIVERY
1-800-940-7678
CALL TODAY!

LATE CITY FINAL

SATURDAY, JULY 5, 1997 / Sunny, 85 / Weather: Page 12 ★★   http://www.nypostonline.com/ · · · · 50¢

EARTH
- Spaceship lands safely
- Search for life begins

INVADES MARS

FULL STORY PLUS PHOTO: PAGE 7

Dog-day afternoon

Champion Hirofumi Nakajima of Japan flashes a thumbs-up sign after he set a world record by swallowing 24 1/2 hot dogs in 12 minutes to successfully defend his title in the Nathan's contest in Coney Island yesterday. Ed Krachie (left) of Queens could only agonize over his defeat.

INDEPENDENCE DAY CELEBRATIONS: PAGES 4 & 5

Earth Invades Mars

For decades, Hollywood movies have presented alien visitors from outer space as everything from friendly childlike creatures and philanthropists to ferocious colonizers intent on destroying the earth and everything on it.

This time, however, it was Earth's turn to play visitor as the *Pathfinder* spacecraft completed a seven-month journey, landing on the Red Planet equipped with the first-ever robotic rover, the Sojourner, and a camera with relay capabilities—providing humans the first crystal clear views of the Martian surface.

No aliens, no canals—but most definitely red.

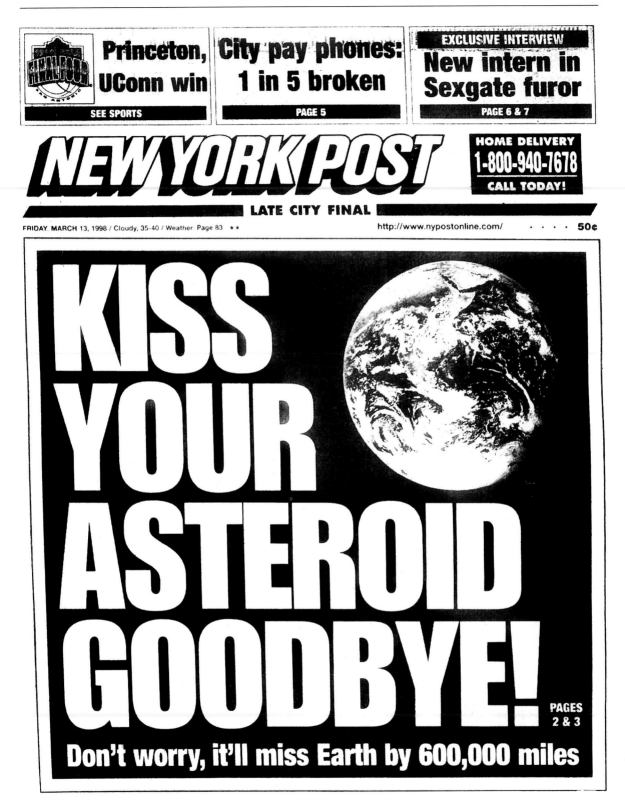

Princeton, UConn win
SEE SPORTS

City pay phones: 1 in 5 broken
PAGE 5

EXCLUSIVE INTERVIEW
New intern in Sexgate furor
PAGE 6 & 7

NEW YORK POST

HOME DELIVERY
1-800-940-7678
CALL TODAY!

LATE CITY FINAL

FRIDAY, MARCH 13, 1998 / Cloudy, 35-40 / Weather: Page 83 ★ ★   http://www.nypostonline.com/   · · · · **50¢**

KISS YOUR ASTEROID GOODBYE!

PAGES 2 & 3

Don't worry, it'll miss Earth by 600,000 miles

Pregnant Uma may wed Ethan Hawke

PAGE 7

Uma Thurman

Yankees, Mets win at Shea

PAGE 3 & SPORTS

NEW YORK POST

HOME DELIVERY
1-800-940-7678
CALL TODAY!

LATE CITY FINAL

THURSDAY, APRIL 16, 1998 / Afternoon showers, low 60s / Weather: Page 46   ★★   http://www.nypostonline.com/   · · · ·   50¢

Oliver@cybersex.con:

YOU'VE GOT JAIL!

Oliver Jovanovic faces 25 years to life for cybersex conviction.

COMPLETE COVERAGE BEGINS ON PAGES 4 & 5

30 seconds from disaster
Near-miss over Giants Stadium
PAGE 7

Last-minute guide to New Year's
FULL COVERAGE STARTS ON PAGE 3

NEW YORK POST

**HOME DELIVERY
1-800-940-7678
CALL TODAY!**

LATE CITY FINAL

THURSDAY, DECEMBER 31, 1998 / Partly cloudy and cold, 30 / Weather: Page 26   ★★

http://www.nypost.com/

50¢

UNDER MOUSE ARREST

Dunkin' Donuts closes rodent-infested shop, will probe 30 others

FULL STORY ON PAGE 5

RAGIN' RUDY / Hizzoner takes off the gloves
PAGE 4

Why Caroline shuns the Kennedy clan

PAGES 28 & 29

NEW YORK POST

HOME DELIVERY
1-800-552-7678
CALL TODAY!

LATE CITY FINAL

WEDNESDAY, JULY 28, 1999 / Sunny and warm, 88-93 / Weather: Page 73 ★★   http://www.nypost.com/   • 50¢

NUDESTOCK

Troopers probed for posing with naked rock fans

PAGE 3

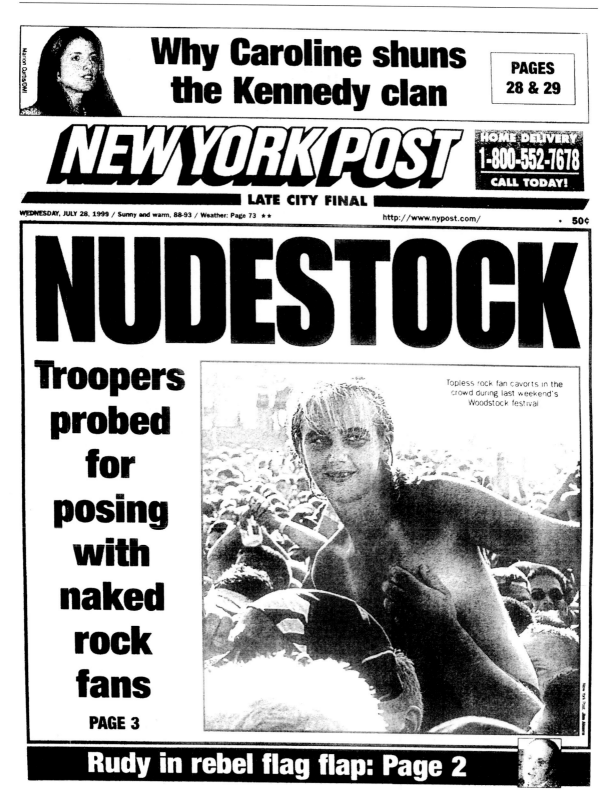

Topless rock fan cavorts in the crowd during last weekend's Woodstock festival

Rudy in rebel flag flap: Page 2

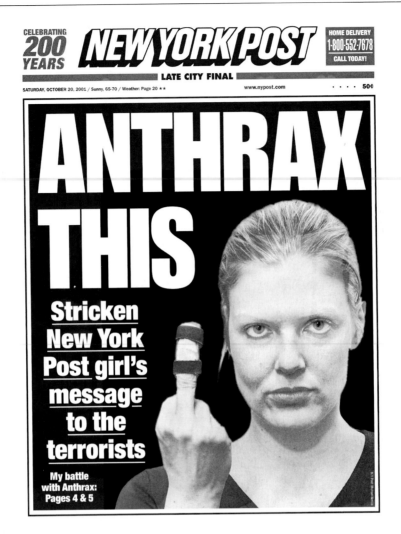

NEW YORK POST

LATE CITY FINAL

SATURDAY, OCTOBER 20, 2001 / Sunny, 65-70 / Weather: Page 20 ★★   www.nypost.com   · · · · 50¢

ANTHRAX THIS

Stricken New York Post girl's message to the terrorists

My battle with Anthrax: Pages 4 & 5

Anthrax This

As administrative assistant for *The Post*'s editorial and op-ed pages, Johanna Huden was always looking for a way to launch a writing career. Just a couple of weeks after 9/11, she found it—big time.

Huden was the first person to be infected with anthrax spores sent through the mail to various media outlets, including *The Post*. As her story became public, she wrote, "I was on the *Fox News* ticker, a mob of reporters was down on Sixth Avenue, waiting, and the mayor was holding a press conference—about me!"

Fortunately, the worst that Huden suffered was a badly infected finger; in contrast, several people exposed to the lethal spores in separate circumstances actually died. Two other *Post* employees were infected, but neither became seriously ill.

And it was inevitable that, given which of Huden's fingers was infected—coupled with the fact that, once wrapped in gauze, it was forced to remain extended—she'd wind up on Page One delivering an undeniable message to her attackers.

Luckily, she got through the ordeal hardly the worse for wear. Her finger healed, and the photo on *The Post*'s front page became an iconic message that made her instantly recognizable.

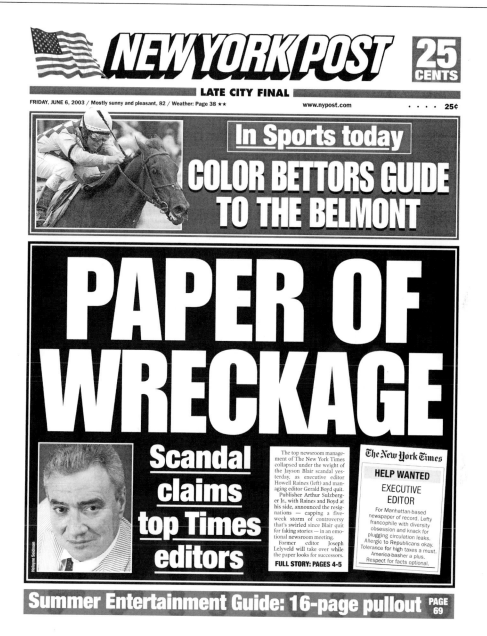

NEW YORK POST

25 CENTS

LATE CITY FINAL

FRIDAY, JUNE 6, 2003 / Mostly sunny and pleasant, 82 / Weather: Page 38 ★★   www.nypost.com   · · · · 25¢

In Sports today

COLOR BETTORS GUIDE TO THE BELMONT

PAPER OF WRECKAGE

Scandal claims top Times editors

The top newsroom management of The New York Times collapsed under the weight of the Jayson Blair scandal yesterday, as executive editor Howell Raines (left) and managing editor Gerald Boyd quit.

Publisher Arthur Sulzberger Jr, with Raines and Boyd at his side, announced the resignations — capping a five-week storm of controversy that's swirled since Blair quit for faking stories — in an emotional newsroom meeting.

Former editor Joseph Lelyveld will take over while the paper looks for successors.

FULL STORY: PAGES 4-5

The New York Times

HELP WANTED

EXECUTIVE EDITOR

For Manhattan-based newspaper of record. Lefty francophile with diversity obsession and knack for plugging circulation leaks. Allergic to Republicans okay. Tolerance for high taxes a must. America-basher a plus. Respect for facts optional.

Summer Entertainment Guide: 16-page pullout PAGE 69

Paper of Wreckage

Big-city dailies form natural rivalries that make them better than they would otherwise be.

But the *New York Times* is sui generis; its only meaningful morning rival—the late and lamented *Herald Tribune*—expired in 1966.

At that point, the *Times* disengaged from the city and evolved into the snooty and self-styled "Paper of record."

So when things began to unravel amid the Jayson Blair scandal, it was the most natural thing in the world to label it "Paper of Wreckage."

The late, great New York Giants owner Wellington Mara once remarked on a Dallas Cowboys loss: "It's nice to see arrogance humbled."

We know the feeling.

NEW YORK POST

LATE CITY FINAL

25 CENTS

MONDAY, JUNE 14, 2004 / Cloudy, chance of rain, 79 / Weather: Page 37 ★★ R   www.nypost.com   · · · · 25¢

N.Y. Post: Mary McLoughlin

Cup & gown

Breast jobs new grad fad for girls

EXCLUSIVE: PAGE 7

Heather Panzner did so well in school, she convinced her folks to shell out $6,750 for a boob job for graduation.

DERAILED

Cops nab serial train hijacker

Notorious Darius McCollum (right), who has made a career out of stealing city subways and buses while posing as a transit worker, has been arrested again, this time for walking through a Queens rail yard carrying access keys. His high jinks have highlighted alarming lapses in the MTA's post-9/11 security efforts. McCollum had been paroled from prison for less than three months when the MTA busted him Friday.

FULL STORY: PAGE 5

Brendan Bannon

Yanks spoil Wells' return to The Bronx   SEE SPORTS

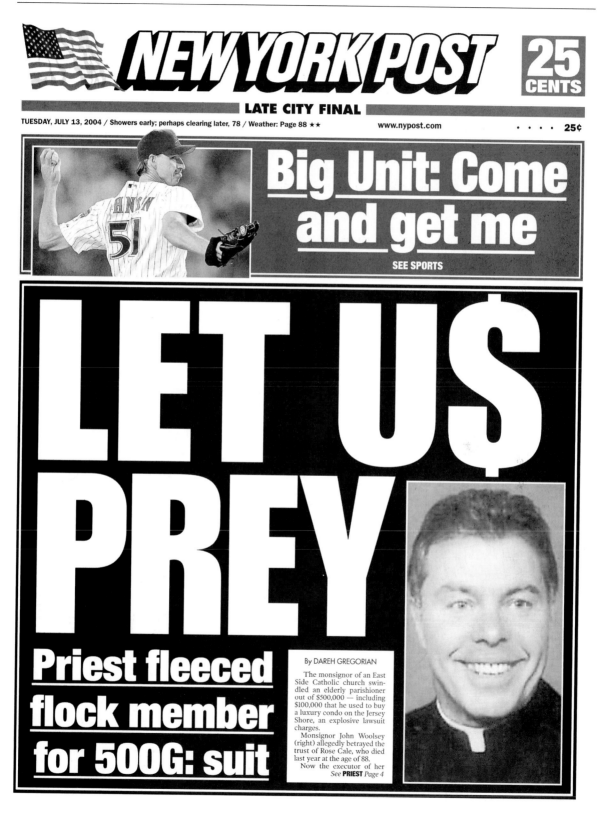

NEW YORK POST

LATE CITY FINAL

TUESDAY, JULY 13, 2004 / Showers early; perhaps clearing later, 78 / Weather: Page 88 ★★   www.nypost.com   · · · · · 25¢

25 CENTS

Big Unit: Come and get me

SEE SPORTS

LET U$ PREY

Priest fleeced flock member for 500G: suit

By DAREH GREGORIAN

The monsignor of an East Side Catholic church swindled an elderly parishioner out of $500,000 — including $100,000 that he used to buy a luxury condo on the Jersey Shore, an explosive lawsuit charges.

Monsignor John Woolsey (right) allegedly betrayed the trust of Rose Cale, who died last year at the age of 88.

Now the executor of her

See **PRIEST** Page 4

SATURDAY, NOVEMBER 13, 2004 / Snow and rain ending early; windy, cold, 43 / Weather: Page 20   www.nypost.com   · · · · · 50¢

NEW YORK POST

ONLY 50¢

METRO EDITION

Scott Peterson guilty

FREY HIM!

Amber Frey   Laci Peterson

Now faces death penalty

Scott Peterson

FULL STORY: PAGES 2, 3, 4, 5

Runaway Bride

Jennifer Wilbanks wasn't the first young woman ever to go missing. But something about the wild-eyed photo that flashed across the nation's newspapers and TV screens gripped many Americans—especially after it was learned that she'd phoned home, reporting she'd been kidnapped and sexually assaulted. The story got even better when, three days later, she turned up safe and sound and admitted the whole thing had been a hoax. In fact, the 32-year-old Duluth, Ga., woman had only been having second thoughts about getting married and needed some time to think.

"Flee-ancée" was an obvious pun. But as the second headline suggested, Wilbanks' cold feet were about to land her in some legal hot water—she would later be indicted for making false statements to police and agree to reimburse her local police department $13,000 in costs related to her search.

The last headline accompanied The Post's exclusive that revealed the real reason Wilbanks fled: Her fiancée, a self-confessed "born-again virgin," was insisting on total sexual abstinence until they were married—and she just couldn't take it anymore.

NEW YORK POST

LATE CITY FINAL

25 CENTS

MONDAY, MAY 2, 2005 / Partly sunny, late showers, 60-64 / Weather: Page 20 ★★   www.nypost.com   • • • • 25¢

Yankees™ Immortals Medallions

NEW YORK YANKEES™
ROGER MARIS

ROGER MARIS COUPON TODAY

SEE BACK PAGE

THE RUNAWAY BRIDE

COLD FEET, HOT WATER

Jennifer Wilbanks and jilted John Mason.

Jiltin' Jenny could face 5 years in jail

Georgia cops yesterday threatened to slap a felony rap on bolting bride Jennifer Wilbanks if her premarital escape was premeditated. That could land her in jail for five years. A crucial detail is the Greyhound bus ticket she reportedly bought up to a week before she fled.

FULL STORY: PAGES 4 & 5

GREYHOUND

NEW YORK POST

ONLY
50¢

METRO EDITION

FRIDAY, MAY 6, 2005 / Some sunshine giving way to clouds, 62 / Weather: Page 67   www.nypost.com   · · · ·   **50¢**

Kentucky Derby
COLOR BETTOR'S GUIDE

RUNAWAY BRIDE'S SECRET

COLD SHEETS

Jennifer Wilbanks has a good *sexcuse* for her cross-country bolt from the altar — her fiancé isn't giving her any.

Friends of the runaway bride said the fun-loving 32-year-old, who once had a very active dating life, is upset her hubby-to-be has adopted a policy of abstaining before marriage.

STORY: PAGE 5 & ANDREA PEYSER

Jen jilted 'no sex' beau

Sizzling Piazza powers Mets   SEE SPORTS

New York Post

METRO EDITION

ONLY 50¢

TUESDAY, MAY 17, 2005 / Sunshine mixing with clouds and cool, 68 / Weather: Page 30 · · · · www.nypost.com · · · · **50¢**

Israel in crisis over Madonna

PAGE 7

Star Wars zapped my love life

PAGE 3

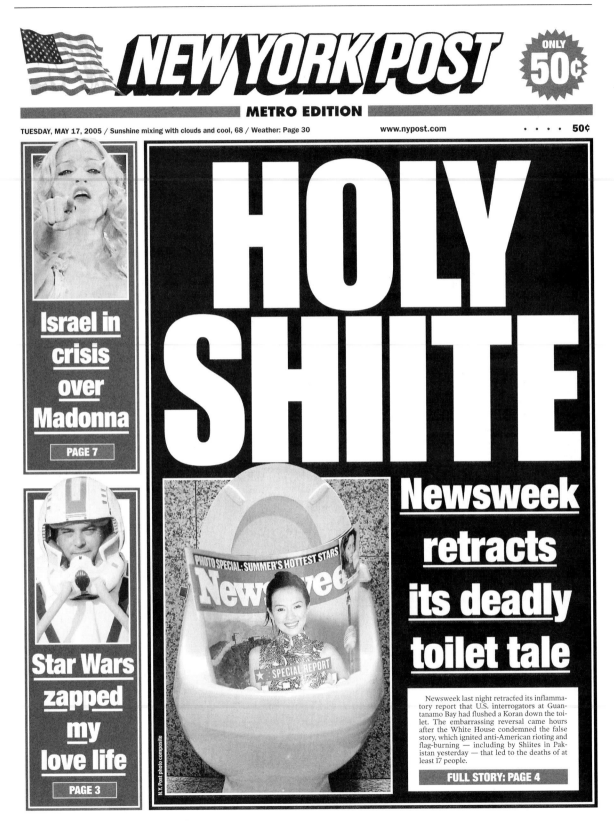

N.Y. Post photo composite

HOLY SHIITE

Newsweek retracts its deadly toilet tale

Newsweek last night retracted its inflammatory report that U.S. interrogators at Guantanamo Bay had flushed a Koran down the toilet. The embarrassing reversal came hours after the White House condemned the false story, which ignited anti-American rioting and flag-burning — including by Shiites in Pakistan yesterday — that led to the deaths of at least 17 people.

FULL STORY: PAGE 4

NEW YORK POST

LATE CITY FINAL

25 CENTS

TUESDAY, MAY 24, 2005 / Mostly cloudy, a shower in spots; cooler, 58 / Weather: Page 66 ★★   www.nypost.com   · · · · 25¢

QUACK IS BACK

Killer doc finally to face justice

A phony doctor who allegedly botched surgery on a banker — then buried her butchered body in his yard — is back in New York after fleeing to Costa Rica. Dean Faiello, here in cuffs at JFK yesterday, is accused of killing Maria Cruz (right) in 2003.

FULL STORY: PAGE 5

Josh Williams

NEW YORK POST

LATE CITY FINAL

25 CENTS

FRIDAY, NOVEMBER 4, 2005 / Mostly sunny, breezy and warm, 72 / Weather: Page 87 ★★   www.nypost.com   · · · ·   25¢

iPorn

SEE STORY PAGE 3

Steamy streaming video for iPod

MENU

PLANE CRAZY

Fliers fear bid to OK knives

Air passengers turned white-knuckled yesterday over word the feds might ease post-9/11 restrictions to allow travelers to bring scissors and small knives aboard planes again.

"I'd like to know why [knives] are no longer a threat when they were a threat over the last four years," fumed Queens Rep. Joseph Crowley, whose firefighter cousin died on Sept. 11.

STORY: PAGE 2

NEW YORK POST

ONLY 50¢

METRO EDITION

TUESDAY, JANUARY 3, 2006 / Wet snow mixing in; windy and raw, 41 / Weather: Page 22   www.nypost.com   · · · ·   50¢

FACE OF TERROR

Err-port security bars tot

EXCLUSIVE

This adorable kid wouldn't harm a fly — but the feds fear 4-year-old Edward Allen is a terrorist. Security officials at La Guardia and in Houston tried to block Edward — here with mom Sijollie — from boarding after his name popped up on the no-fly terror watch list.

FULL STORY: PAGE 3

Nathan Lindstrom

10 reasons Giants will win

STEVE SERBY IN SPORTS

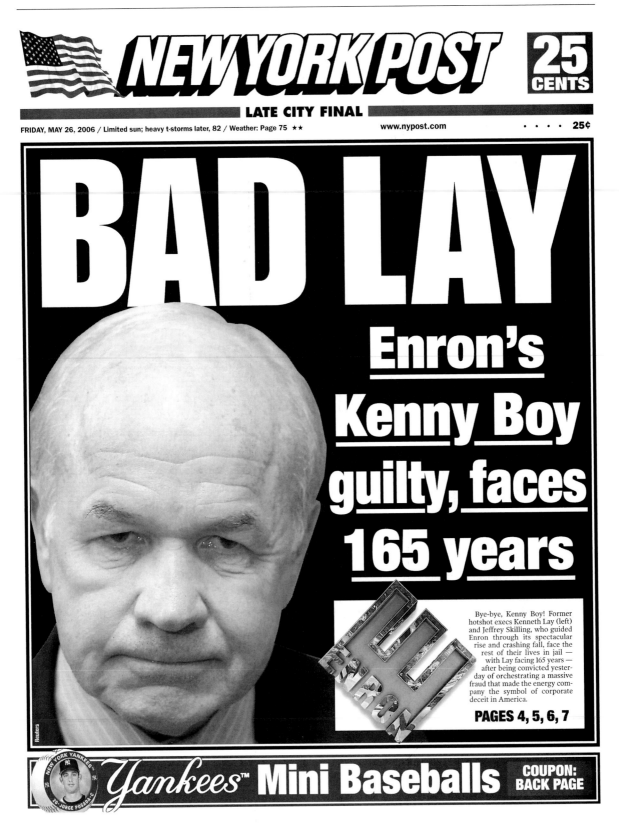

NEW YORK POST

25 CENTS

LATE CITY FINAL

FRIDAY, MAY 26, 2006 / Limited sun; heavy t-storms later, 82 / Weather: Page 75 ★★   www.nypost.com   · · · · 25¢

BAD LAY

Enron's Kenny Boy guilty, faces 165 years

Bye-bye, Kenny Boy! Former hotshot execs Kenneth Lay (left) and Jeffrey Skilling, who guided Enron through its spectacular rise and crashing fall, face the rest of their lives in jail — with Lay facing 165 years — after being convicted yesterday of orchestrating a massive fraud that made the energy company the symbol of corporate deceit in America.

PAGES 4, 5, 6, 7

Reuters

Yankees™ **Mini Baseballs**   COUPON: BACK PAGE

NEW YORK POST

25 CENTS

LATE CITY FINAL

MONDAY, AUGUST 21, 2006 / Mostly sunny, 86 / Weather: Page 22 ★★ RR   www.nypost.com   • • • • 25¢

SNAKE ON A PLANE

JonBenet 'killer' lands in U.S. jail

JONBENET MURDER

Talk about air pollution. Creepy teacher John Mark Karr, the self-professed killer of JonBenet Ramsey, sits aboard a flight from Thailand back to the United States yesterday. And he flew in style, sipping champagne and dining on king prawns as he sat in business class.

But when the jet landed early this morning in Los Angeles, the kiddie-sex pervert was taken straight to a local jail, pending an extradition hearing for his eventual trip to Colorado to face murder charges in the infamous 1996 slaying of the 6-year-old beauty queen.

SEE PAGES 4, 5 & 6

AP

Tiger stalks off with PGA crown SEE SPORTS

Snake on a Plane

The Post doesn't get knocked around much for helping create the "tabloid mentality"—mainly because it has become the mainstream.

After all, what *is* news? It's what people talk about, what engages them.

The Post, therefore, went hell-for-leather on nut-job John Mark Karr, who convinced a putatively responsible justice system that he was present for the murder of JonBenet Ramsey.

But unlike the erstwhile "major networks," we gave it exactly the treatment it deserved.

Incidentally, the wonderful line "Snake on a Plane" did not come from the desk; it came from reporter Dan Mangan. That doesn't happen a lot, but it isn't coincidental that every editor on the copy desk used to be a reporter.

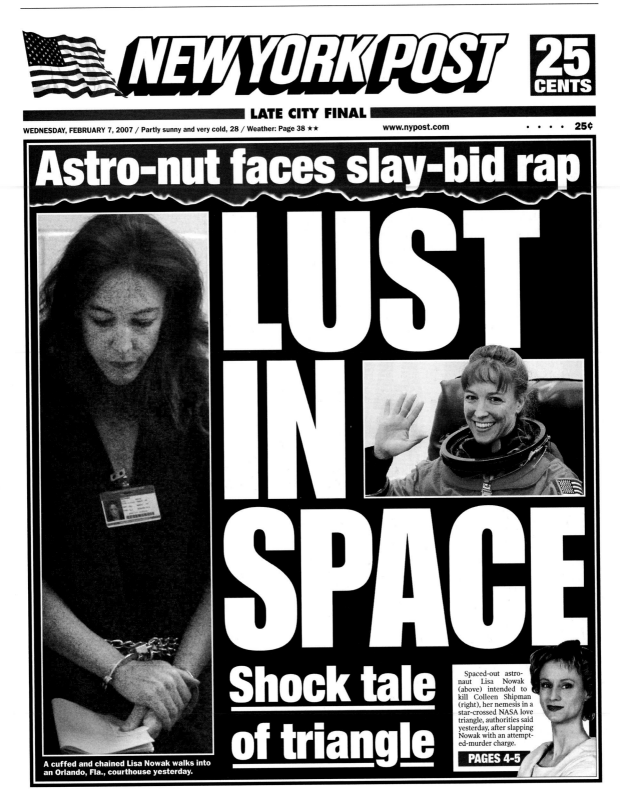

NEW YORK POST

25 CENTS

LATE CITY FINAL

WEDNESDAY, FEBRUARY 7, 2007 / Partly sunny and very cold, 28 / Weather: Page 38 ★★   www.nypost.com   • • • • 25¢

Astro-nut faces slay-bid rap

LUST IN SPACE

Shock tale of triangle

A cuffed and chained Lisa Nowak walks into an Orlando, Fla., courthouse yesterday.

Spaced-out astronaut Lisa Nowak (above) intended to kill Colleen Shipman (right), her nemesis in a star-crossed NASA love triangle, authorities said yesterday, after slapping Nowak with an attempted-murder charge.

PAGES 4-5

NEW YORK POST

LATE CITY FINAL

SATURDAY, MAY 26, 2007 / Sunshine, 90 / Weather: Page 41 ★★   www.nypost.com   · · · · 50¢

Jurassic Pork

KID HUNTER BAGS HUGE HOG: PAGE 3

CASH BASH

Feisty Boss: Brian's 'on the hook'

Yankees' boss George Steinbrenner yesterday fired a warning shot in the direction of General Manager Brian Cashman, saying that he "needs to deliver" as the struggling Bombers try to right their shaky season.

SEE SPORTS

AP

POLITICS

New York Post

FOUNDED 1801 THE OLDEST CONTINUOUSLY PUBLISHED DAILY IN THE UNITED STATES

NEW YORK, FRIDAY, SEPTEMBER 17, 1976   25 Cents

CLOSING MARKET FINAL 6 RACES

WEATHER
Tonight
Showers, 60s.
Tomorrow chance
of showers, 70s.
Sunny Sunday
Air Good

NEW TAX BILL HITS BETTORS

Perils OTB, Tracks, Lottery

By Ralph Blumenfeld

The tax bill now on President Ford's desk contains a little-publicized provision that would require anyone winning $1000 or more in legal betting to pay an immediate 20 per cent with-holding tax to the Internal Revenue Service.

Racetrack and Off Track Betting Corp officials here called the bill "devastating" to legal horse racing and said it would drive bettors to bookies.

The bill also could have serious consequences for the New York State Lottery.

OTB president Paul Screvane, describing the measure as "the rip-off of all time," said it would "create chaos at parimutuel ticket windows both on and off tracks."

Saying the provision penalized winners of $1000 or more, he said:

"Nobody will buy a $100 ticket again. They'll get 50 $2 tickets and cash them at different windows."

Arnold Kirkpatrick of the American Horse Council said:

"This is going to be devastating. This is going to drive everybody right to the bookies."

If a horseplayer bets $500 on a 2-to-1 shot and wins, $200 of his $1000 profits will be with-held at the cashier's window.

It appeared, however, that a bettor could beat the tax by cashing smaller tickets at different windows or having others cash some.

Continued on Page 65

RETURNING THE COMPLIMENT: Vice President Rockefeller replies in kind to the gestures of some student hecklers during a stop in Binghamton with Sen. Robert Dole. See Judith Michaelson, Page 4.

Rockefeller Flipping the Bird

People couldn't believe their eyes as they passed the city's newsstands one afternoon in September 1976. Was that really the vice president of the United States, Nelson Rockefeller, flipping the bird on Page One of *The Post*?

It happened in upstate Binghamton, where the former governor of New York was campaigning on behalf of Sen. Bob Dole, who was running for Rockefeller's job on the GOP ticket headed by President Gerald Ford. Rocky found himself being harangued by a crowd of college students over the 1971 Attica prison riot, in which 38 people were killed.

"Attica killer" and "Any way you figure, Rocky pulled the trigger" were just some of the cries leveled at the veep. Undaunted, he countered by introducing Dole as a candidate who'd fought in World War II for the right of young people to protest. They responded by raising their middle fingers en masse. To everyone's amazement, Rockefeller cheerfully responded in kind.

The Post was one of the few papers to publish the photo at all, let alone on the front page. Friends and supporters were horrified; rumors spread that he had a drinking problem. But as one aide noted: "He drinks that sweet stuff, Dubonnet sherry—you can't get drunk on that."

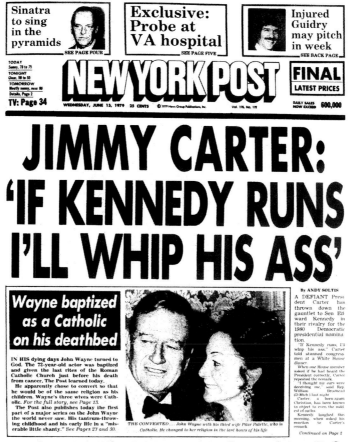

Jimmy Carter: "If Kennedy Runs I'll Whip His Ass"

The two congressmen who heard the president of the United States couldn't believe their ears and asked him to repeat it. And when *The Post* splashed the quote across Page One, the collective jaw of the rest of the news media dropped as well.

Jimmy Carter made his confident (and accurate) prediction to two Democratic congressmen, William Brodhead of Michigan and Tom Downey of New York, at a White House dinner. "I'm sorry, Mr. President," said Brodhead. "I'm not quite sure I understood you." So Carter repeated the remark.

It first appeared in print in the *Washington Post* under the headline: "Carter Reported to Say He Would Beat Kennedy." Somehow, the story didn't attract any attention—until the *New York Post* followed up with its attention-grabbing front page.

That night, the story led all the major network news broadcasts. CBS substitute anchor Bob Schieffer opened his broadcast by flashing a photo of *The Post*'s front page, saying: "If you thought Billy Carter (the president's colorful redneck brother) was the most quotable member of the Carter family, check out this headline."

Kennedy's response: "I knew the White House was standing behind me. I just didn't realize how closely."

Star Wars in Action!

When President Ronald Reagan proposed what he called the Strategic Defense Initiative—ground- and space-based systems that would defend the United States against incoming ballistic nuclear missiles—it seemed like something of science fiction.

Post editors quickly reached for an easy-to-remember term, taken from the era's most popular movie, that summed up the plan in an instant—the next day's front page described the plan simply as "Star Wars."

The phrase took root. Soon everyone, including White House officials, was referring to the plan as "Star Wars." And it all began on the front page of the *New York Post*.

We preview 3 **BIG** movies

EBERT & MUSETTO PAGE 37

NEW YORK POST

SPORTS FINAL

TONIGHT: Partly cloudy, windy, mid 20s.
TOMORROW: Partly sunny, breezy, mid 30s. Details: Page 2

WEDNESDAY, DEC. 16, 1987   *Founded by Alexander Hamilton in 1801*   35 CENTS

HART TO BELIEVE!

Gary tosses monkey wrench into race

In and out Democratic presidential hopeful Gary Hart was in the campaign again yesterday as he joked with Popeye in Concord, N.H. — but the ghost of cavorting on the good ship Monkey Business with Donna Rice (above) in Bimini was lurking in the background. Hart dropped a blockbuster on the '88 race and reentered the fray yesterday after pulling out last May in the wake of a scandal involving Rice.

New York Post: Paul Adao

Full coverage starts PAGES 4 & 5

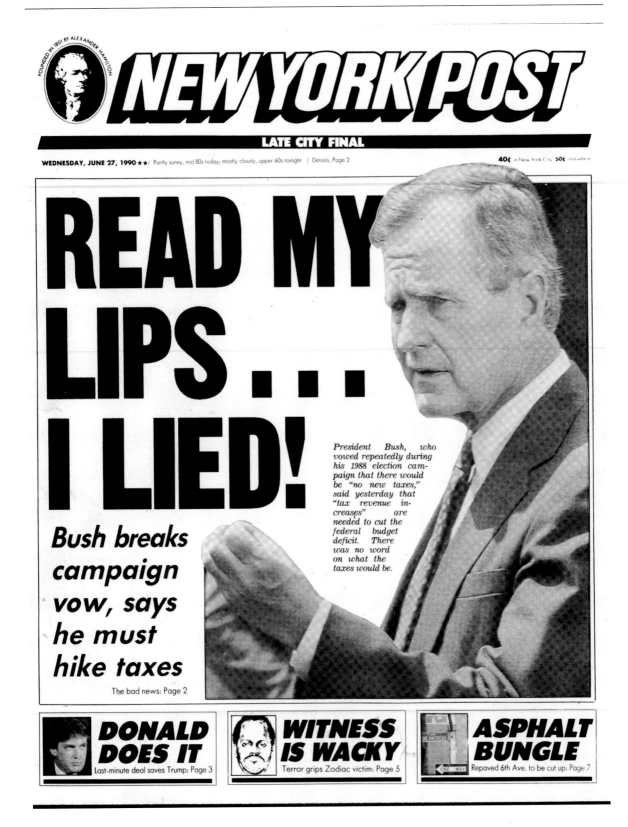

FOUNDED IN 1801 BY ALEXANDER HAMILTON

NEW YORK POST

LATE CITY FINAL

WEDNESDAY, JUNE 27, 1990 ★★/ Partly sunny, mid 80s today; mostly cloudy, upper 60s tonight / Details, Page 2

40¢ in New York City 50¢ elsewhere

READ MY LIPS ... I LIED!

Bush breaks campaign vow, says he must hike taxes

The bad news: Page 2

President Bush, who vowed repeatedly during his 1988 election campaign that there would be "no new taxes," said yesterday that "tax revenue increases" are needed to cut the federal budget deficit. There was no word on what the taxes would be.

DONALD DOES IT
Last-minute deal saves Trump: Page 3

WITNESS IS WACKY
Terror grips Zodiac victim: Page 5

ASPHALT BUNGLE
Repaved 6th Ave. to be cut up: Page 7

FOUNDED IN 1801 BY ALEXANDER HAMILTON

NEW YORK POST

LATE CITY FINAL

FRIDAY, NOVEMBER 15, 1991 ★★ / Cloudy, low 60s today; chance of showers, low 40s tonight / Details, Page 2

40¢ in New York City 50¢ elsewhere

Gubernatorial candidate David Duke, an ex-Klansman, on the stump in Lafayette, La.

Associated Press

AmeriKKKan nightmare

Will David Duke win in Louisiana?

See Page 5

FERRARO THROWS HAT IN SENATE RING Page Four

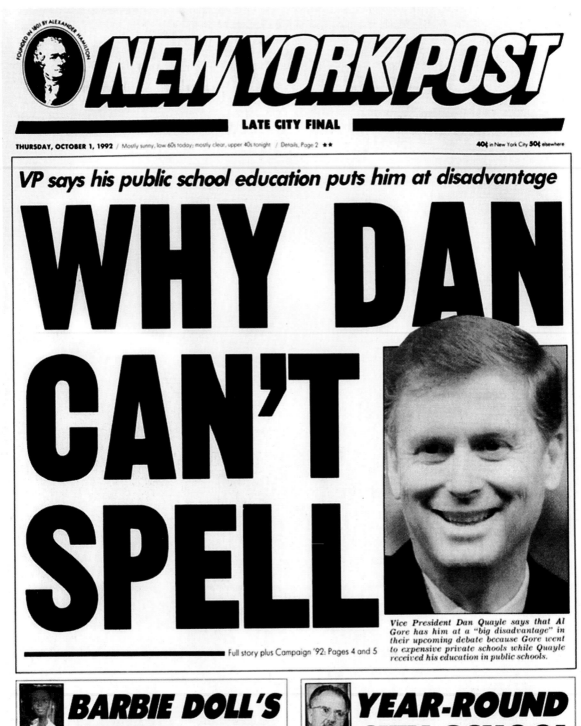

LATE CITY FINAL

THURSDAY, OCTOBER 1, 1992 / Mostly sunny, low 60s today; mostly clear, upper 40s tonight / Details, Page 2 ★ ★

40¢ in New York City 50¢ elsewhere

VP says his public school education puts him at disadvantage

WHY DAN CAN'T SPELL

Full story plus Campaign '92: Pages 4 and 5

Vice President Dan Quayle says that Al Gore has him at a "big disadvantage" in their upcoming debate because Gore went to expensive private schools while Quayle received his education in public schools.

BARBIE DOLL'S SEXIST SLUR

Find out what the talking toy said: Page 4

YEAR-ROUND CITY SCHOOL

Fernandez plan in the works — EXCLUSIVE: Page 3

Empire State shooter plotted rampage a year

FULL COVERAGE STARTS ON PAGES 2 & 3

Wall Street may fuel $2B state tax windfall

PAGE 5

NEW YORK POST

HOME DELIVERY
1-800-940-7678
CALL TODAY!

LATE CITY FINAL

WEDNESDAY, FEBRUARY 26, 1997 / Sun and clouds, 48-53 / Weather: Page 24 ★★   http://www.nypostonline.com/   · · · **50¢**

BILL'S BED AND BREAKFAST

The Clintons played host to 938 people during the President's first term. Now, new documents show he ordered aides to court fat-cat donors by offering overnight stays and private meetings with him.

Prez personally ordered White House sleepovers to woo big-bucks donors

FULL COVERAGE STARTS ON PAGES 6 & 7

Giuliani to Brits:

POOH ON YOU!

Mayor Giuliani is steamed that Great Britain wants the original Winnie the Pooh doll, inspiration for the animated character, back from the New York Public Library.

Trans-Atlantic battle over original 'Winnie' dolls   PAGES 4 & 5

AIR BETSY?

Lt. gov.'s hubby may bail out ailing Pan Am

Betsy McCaughey Ross

PAGE 2

NEW YORK POST

DAILY 35¢

LATE CITY FINAL

SATURDAY, FEBRUARY 28, 1998 / Morning sun, afternoon rain, 55 / Weather: Page 37 ★★   http://www.nypost.com/ · · · ·

Latest spin control from the White House:

THEY ONLY KISSED!

— and Monica exaggerated

FULL STORY: PAGE 6

NEW YORK POST

LATE CITY FINAL

FRIDAY, AUGUST 7, 1998 / Partly sunny, 85 / Weather: Page 70 ★★   http://www.nypost.com/   · · · · 50¢

Rivera

Geraldo shocker: 'I want Brokaw's job'

PAGE 7

Mets walk to another win

SEE SPORTS

Peter Pan statue rescued from river

PAGE 6

THE FULL MONICA

Lewinsky tells grand jury of more than a dozen sex encounters with prez: report

COMPLETE COVERAGE BEGINS ON PAGE 2

Associated Press

House panel cites Reno for contempt

PAGE 8

Straw's rallying cry for cancer-stricken Torre

'WIN IT FOR THE SKIPPER'

PAGES 4-5

Joe Torre

NEW YORK POST

HOME DELIVERY
1-800-552-7678
CALL TODAY!

LATE CITY FINAL

THURSDAY, MARCH 11, 1999 / Sunny and cool, 40-45 / Weather: Page 59 ★★   http://www.nypost.com/   · · · · **50¢**

CHILLARY

'I don't want to be in the same room with him, let alone the same bed.'

— *TV news report quoting Hillary Clinton on the state of her marriage*

PAGES 2-3

Hillary Clinton reportedly cut short the First Couple's skiing vacation and skipped the presidential tour of Latin America because of new strains in their relationship.

Associated Press File Photo

Chinese OK new diplo-crew visit
PAGE 7

Rudy's 'Jihad' on Hevesi: is it real?
PAGE 4

Bulls roar, stocks soar
PAGE 2

CELEBRATING
200 YEARS

NEW YORK POST

25 CENTS

LATE CITY FINAL

FRIDAY, APRIL 6, 2001 / Cloudy & cooler with showers, 54 / Weather: Page 66 ★★   www.nypost.com   25¢

HILL NO!

Clinton says she'll NEVER run for prez

PAGE 3

200 YEARS
NEW YORK POST

Be Cinderella for a day
SEE PAGE 61

200 TICKETS

THURSDAY, FEBRUARY 22, 2007 / Mostly cloudy with a couple of showers, 46 / Weather: Page 40 ★★   www.nypost.com   • • • •   25¢

NEW YORK POST

LATE CITY FINAL

25 CENTS

THE BIG CHILL

Starring...

HILLARY CLINTON

DAVID GEFFEN

BARACK OBAMA

AS 'THE WRONGED WOMAN'

AS 'THE DOUBLE-CROSSER'

AS 'THE NEW KID ON THE BLOCK'

H'wood mogul sparks Dems' uncivil war

Like a scene from a bad Hollywood movie, the campaigns of Democratic presidential rivals Hillary Rodham Clinton and Barack Obama exploded into an astonishingly nasty war of words yesterday after film mogul David Geffen trashed his former friends Hill and Bill and raised money for Obama.

PAGES 6-7

HILL GETS NASTY
First lady unleashes her harshest attack yet on Lazio
COMPLETE COVERAGE BEGINS ON PAGES 4 & 5

NEW YORK POST

25 CENTS

LATE CITY FINAL

FRIDAY, NOVEMBER 3, 2000 / A beautiful sunny day, 68 / Weather: Page 28 ★ ★   www.nypost.com   · · · 25¢

■ **Bush: I'm not proud of drunken-driving rap**

■ **Controversy over timing of revelation**

SEE PAGES 2 & 3

A contrite George W. Bush, who has admitted to reckless behavior in his youth, last night acknowledged a 1976 arrest for drunken driving.

D-DUBYA-I

Bomb blast perils Mideast peace talks
PAGES 6 & 7

NEW YORK POST

25 CENTS

LATE CITY FINAL

TUESDAY, DECEMBER 5, 2000 / Partly cloudy & breezy, High near 45 / Weather: Page 24 ★★ R   www.nypost.com   V · · · · 25¢

Twin rulings leave Gore ...

DOWN FOR THE RE-COUNT

Associated Press

ELECTION COVERAGE STARTS ON PAGES 2 & 3

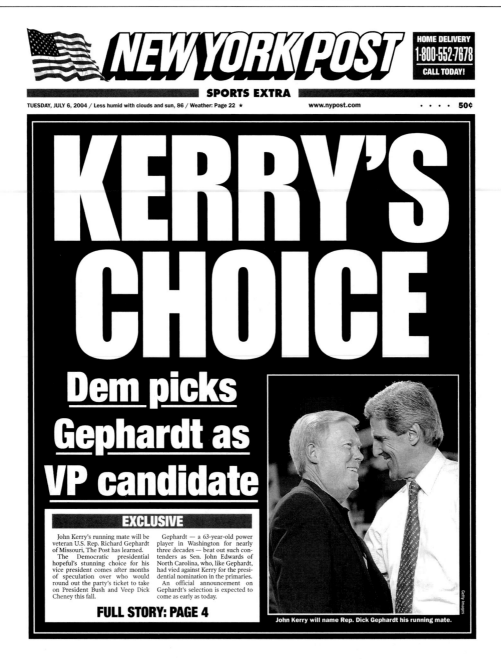

NEW YORK POST

HOME DELIVERY
1-800-552-7678
CALL TODAY!

SPORTS EXTRA

TUESDAY, JULY 6, 2004 / Less humid with clouds and sun, 86 / Weather: Page 22 ★   www.nypost.com   · · · ·   50¢

KERRY'S CHOICE

Dem picks Gephardt as VP candidate

EXCLUSIVE

John Kerry's running mate will be veteran U.S. Rep. Richard Gephardt of Missouri, The Post has learned.

The Democratic presidential hopeful's stunning choice for his vice president comes after months of speculation over who would round out the party's ticket to take on President Bush and Veep Dick Cheney this fall.

Gephardt — a 63-year-old power player in Washington for nearly three decades — beat out such contenders as Sen. John Edwards of North Carolina, who, like Gephardt, had vied against Kerry for the presidential nomination in the primaries.

An official announcement on Gephardt's selection is expected to come as early as today.

FULL STORY: PAGE 4

John Kerry will name Rep. Dick Gephardt his running mate.

Kerry's Choice

This was one of the more embarrassing front pages in *The Post*'s history—a major exclusive that turned out to be completely wrong. Or was it?

Just hours before Democratic presidential nominee John Kerry was to announce his choice of a running mate, *The Post* reported that his selection would be Representative Dick Gephardt of Missouri. But that's not who Kerry named: His candidate was Senator John Edwards of North Carolina.

The Post took it on the chin for that one—though the paper cleverly landed on its feet the following day when it ran the exact same front page, only this time naming Edwards instead of Gephardt.

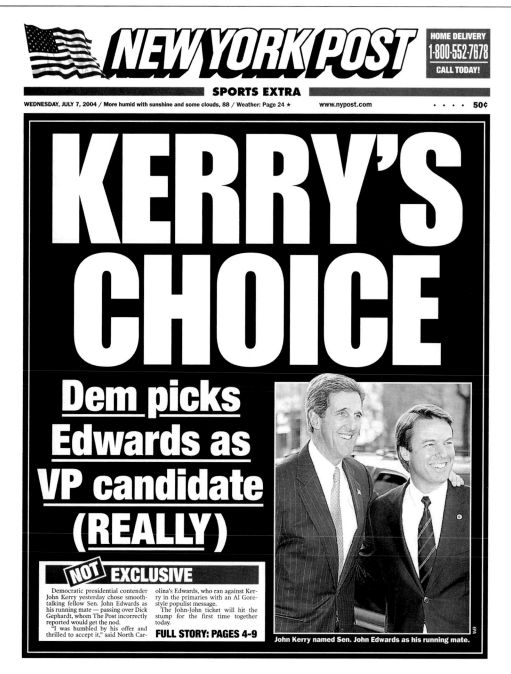

HOME DELIVERY
1-800-552-7678
CALL TODAY!

NEW YORK POST

SPORTS EXTRA

WEDNESDAY, JULY 7, 2004 / More humid with sunshine and some clouds, 88 / Weather: Page 24 ★   www.nypost.com   · · · · 50¢

KERRY'S CHOICE

Dem picks Edwards as VP candidate (REALLY)

NOT EXCLUSIVE

Democratic presidential contender John Kerry yesterday chose smooth-talking fellow Sen. John Edwards as his running mate — passing over Dick Gephardt, whom The Post incorrectly reported would get the nod.

"I was humbled by his offer and thrilled to accept it," said North Car-olina's Edwards, who ran against Kerry in the primaries with an Al Gore-style populist message.

The John-John ticket will hit the stump for the first time together today.

FULL STORY: PAGES 4-9

John Kerry named Sen. John Edwards as his running mate.

But it turns out that the original Page One was pretty close to the mark, and that Dick Gephardt indeed *was* John Kerry's choice for vice president. Problem is, Kerry was apparently convinced by his advisers to change course—after *The Post* had been tipped off to the initial selection.

According to a book by veteran Democratic campaign manager Bob Shrum published in May 2007, Kerry eventually came to regret his selection of Edwards, whom he viewed as a lightweight. Writes Shrum: Kerry "wished that he'd never picked Edwards, that he should have gone with his gut"—and selected Gephardt.

Spaceman Kerry's goofy photo flub

BOSTON, WE HAVE A PROBLEM

By STEFAN C. FRIEDMAN
Post Correspondent

CAPE CANAVERAL — As Democrats kicked off their convention in Boston yesterday, John Kerry broke a cardinal rule of politics — getting his picture taken in a ridiculous outfit.

Kerry resembled a "sperm" (above) in Woody Allen's "Everything You Always Wanted to Know about Sex But Were Afraid to Ask" as he crawled

See **KERRY** Page 6

Boston, We Have a Problem

The moment Republicans saw the photo of Democratic presidential candidate John Kerry wearing a NASA "clean suit," their thoughts jumped gleefully back to 1988. That's when another Democratic White House hopeful, Michael Dukakis, suffered a major hit to his candidacy when he was filmed riding in a tank wearing an oversized helmet—looking to many voters like Mickey Mouse playing war.

This time around, GOP strategists said Kerry resembled comic sperms from Woody Allen's movie *Everything You Always Wanted to Know About Sex (But Were Afraid to Ask.)*

Kerry had other problems that year that cost him the election—but it's probably a good lesson to most candidates: Don't pose for pictures with strange-looking headgear.

Especially when there are great headline writers out there.

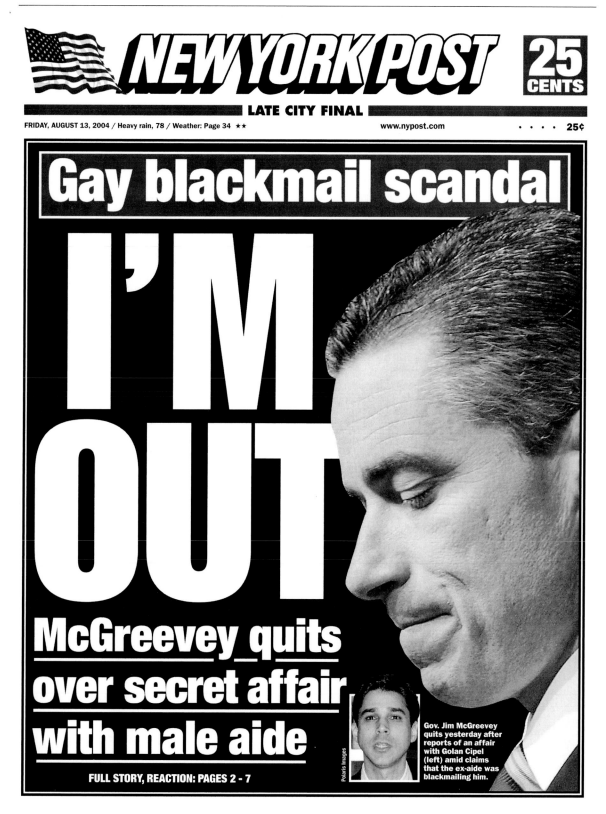

NEW YORK POST

25 CENTS

LATE CITY FINAL

FRIDAY, AUGUST 13, 2004 / Heavy rain, 78 / Weather: Page 34 ★★   www.nypost.com   • • • • 25¢

Gay blackmail scandal

I'M OUT

McGreevey quits over secret affair with male aide

FULL STORY, REACTION: PAGES 2 - 7

Polaris Images

Gov. Jim McGreevey quits yesterday after reports of an affair with Golan Cipel (left) amid claims that the ex-aide was blackmailing him.

NEW YORK POST

25 CENTS

LATE CITY FINAL

WEDNESDAY, SEPTEMBER 1, 2004 / Bright sunny day, 82 / Weather: Page 38 ★★ R   www.nypost.com   · · · · · 25¢

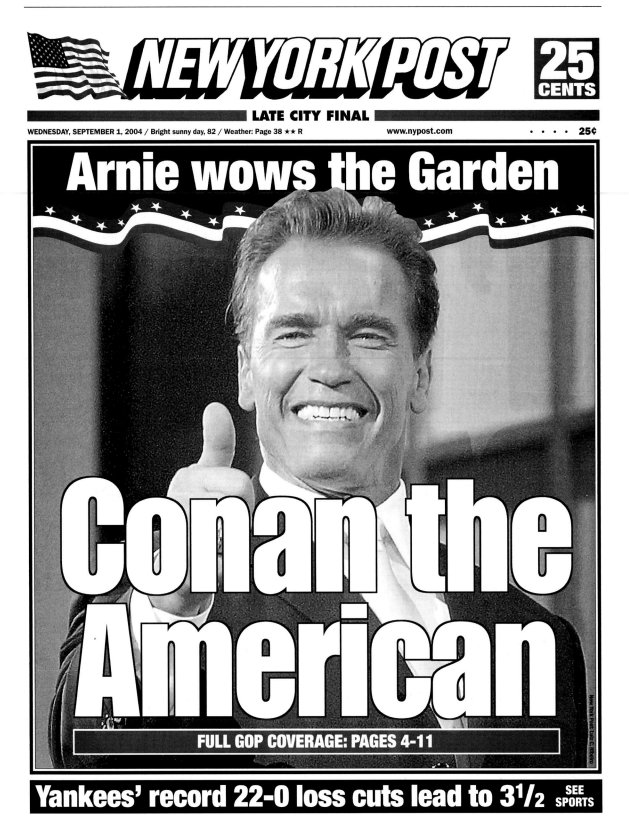

Arnie wows the Garden

Conan the American

FULL GOP COVERAGE: PAGES 4-11

Yankees' record 22-0 loss cuts lead to 3½ SEE SPORTS

NEW YORK POST

ONLY **50¢**

METRO EDITION

THURSDAY, OCTOBER 21, 2004 / Mostly cloudy with some drizzle, 56 / Weather: Page 26   www.nypost.com   · · · · **50¢**

Cabby fined & banned for backing Bush

EXCLUSIVE: PAGE 3

Schilling rips A-Rod

SEE SPORTS

HEINZ IN A PICKLE

Foot-in-mouth Teresa goofs on Laura job jab

Billionaire ketchup heiress Teresa Heinz Kerry (right) got into trouble yesterday when she said Laura Bush has never had a "real job" — even though the first lady worked for years as a school-teacher and librarian. The wife of Democratic nominee John Kerry was forced to quickly apologize, while Bush aides fumed that Mrs. Kerry's remarks were uncalled for.

FULL STORY: PAGE 4

UPI

NEW YORK POST

LATE CITY FINAL

SATURDAY, FEBRUARY 18, 2006 / Windy and colder, 30-34 /   Weather: Page 16 ★★   www.nypost.com   • • • •   50¢

Lindsay's cabaret
EXCLUSIVE PHOTO: PAGE 3

Premiere Magazine/Gilles Bensimon

Hamptons rentals
REAL ESTATE GUIDE

BUCK SHOTS HERE

Cheney victim Birdy Harry shows his face

By DEBORAH ORIN
Bureau Chief

WASHINGTON — The world got its first look (left) at Vice President Dick Cheney's misfire yesterday — the birdshot-marked face of the Texas hunter who held a press conference as he left the hospital.

Shooting-accident victim Harry Whittington yesterday sent his "love" and apologies to his pal Cheney and said he hopes

See **CHENEY** *Page 8*

Bloomberg

NEW YORK POST

25 CENTS

LATE CITY FINAL

TUESDAY, APRIL 25, 2006 / Weather: Storms in the afternoon, 72 / Page 24 ★★   www.nypost.com   · · · · 25¢

WELL HUNG

Unveiled: Bubba's hip new portrait

Hubba Bubba!

Here's Bill Clinton, striking an any-thing-but-presidential pose, in a painting that will hang at the National Portrait Gallery in Washington starting this summer. In this unconventional creation by artist Nelson Shanks, Clinton bears a passing resemblance to former "Night-line" host Ted Koppel and has a hint of a scowl on his face.

The painting will hang as part of the exhibit "America's Presidents."

The other portrait commissioned at the same time features a more-traditional pro-file of then-First Lady Hillary Rodham Clin-ton.

In her painting, now-Sen. Clinton appears to emulate one of her heroes, Susan B. Anthony, in a profile much like the suf-fragette's on the one-dollar coin.

STORY PAGE 7

POST POKER - TODAY'S NUMBERS: PAGE 48

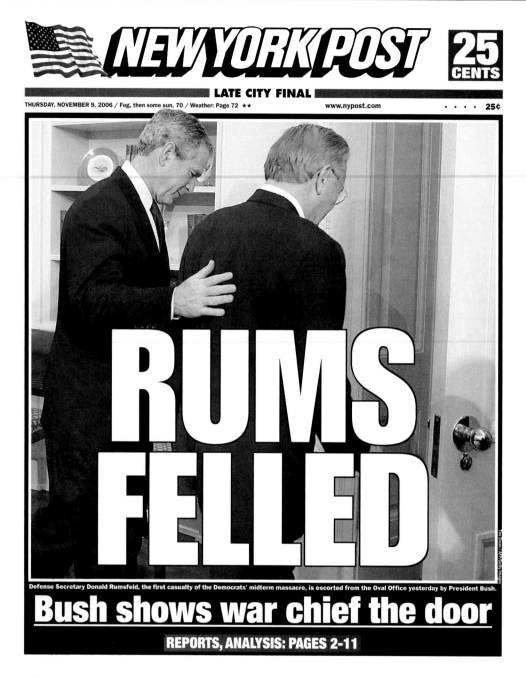

RUMS FELLED

Defense Secretary Donald Rumsfeld, the first casualty of the Democrats' midterm massacre, is escorted from the Oval Office yesterday by President Bush.

Bush shows war chief the door

REPORTS, ANALYSIS: PAGES 2-11

Rums Felled

It would be nice to say we had this one in our back pocket—Donald Rumsfeld had been under siege for a good couple of years.

But we didn't.

It really looked like the secretary of defense wasn't going anywhere; President Bush had been ceaseless in his professions of faith.

But when the administration lost control of Congress and The Other Donald got broomed, we had to think fast.

As for the line itself, sometimes the obvious isn't so obvious. In the end, truncating his name actually worked quite well.

INTERIOR HEADLINES

Salomon big owes us $20M: bank suit

By ERIC LENKOWITZ
and DAREH GREGORIAN

A top executive at Salomon Smith Barney allegedly made more than $160 million of his own money disappear, court papers charge.

Officials at the Bank of New York say in court papers that they discovered Bernard Jaffe's once-bursting bank account is now almost bust when they tried to collect $20 million the Salomon senior vice president for investments owes them.

The bank says in papers filed in Manhattan Supreme Court that it felt safe lending him the whopping sum because his total net worth was over $171 million in 2000.

But at a meeting with bank officials last week, Jaffe said he had only about $7 million left, and when they asked him what had happened to the rest of his fortune, "the only explanation given ... was that the assets were gone."

He "refused to disclose where the assets had gone, to whom they were sold or transferred, or what had happened to the proceeds," the filing says.

Jaffe, 71, and his lawyer, Traci Rollins, didn't return calls for comment.

The bank asked a judge to freeze what's left of the investment chief's cash and property.

According to BoNY's filing, the bank had extended an unsecured line of credit, essentially a collateral-free loan, to Jaffe since 1986. The first year, they gave him a line of $5 million, and, through the years, the amount increased to $20 million.

The bank says it let the missed repayment slide, and agreed to give him until Jan. 15 to repay the $20 million.

But Jaffe, who's worked at Salomon for 45 years, told bank officials at the meeting last Thursday that he's moving to Florida and "couldn't repay the line."

His lawyer said in court papers that her client would eventually repay, but it would take five years "due to extensive financial losses he had suffered over the last year."

When the bank officials asked him what had become of his fortune, he simply told them almost everything was "gone."

The bank has since canceled Jaffe's line of credit, and now wants all its cash back — plus $3,472.22 a day in interest.

BoNY also wants his remaining assets frozen.

BoNY didn't return calls for comment.

ASSASSIN-INE FLUB IN MLK CEREMONY

JAMES EARL JONES
The real man of honor.

JAMES EARL RAY
Murdered MLK in Memphis.

STAMPS ISSUED IN HONOR OF BLACK HERITAGE

Thank you

James Earl Ray

for Keeping the Dream Alive
City of Lauderhill
January 19, 2002

ENGRAVE MISTAKE: This plaque, intended to honor deep-voiced actor James Earl Jones for a Martin Luther King celebration in Florida, was erroneously inscribed with the name of the man who killed the civil-rights leader in 1968.   AP

Plaque accidentally honors killer

By MALCOLM BALFOUR
Post Correspondent

LAUDERHILL, Fla. — City officials had long planned to honor actor James Earl Jones in a Martin Luther King celebration on Saturday.

But they were shocked when they saw the inscription on the plaque they ordered to give him:

"Thank you James Earl Ray for keeping the dream alive."

James Earl Ray is the man who killed King in Memphis in 1968.

Ray pleaded guilty in 1969, but conspiracy theories live on, and now the case of the wrong name is fueling more conspiracy theories.

Jones, an award-winning actor and famous voice heard daily on CNN, as Darth Vader in "Star Wars" films and as Mustafa in "The Lion King," was to receive the plaque as the featured speaker at the King celebration in this city north of Fort Lauderdale this Saturday night.

"This is too terrible for words. It's an outrage," said City Commissioner Margaret Bates, who also heads the city's Martin Luther King task force.

"It's unbelievable that someone could mistakenly confuse James Earl Jones with James Earl Ray the assassin. I'm horrified," she told The Post yesterday.

Members of Bates' task force had commissioned the Lauderhill company Adpro to produce a standard plaque, but later decided to do something special.

Adpro officials suggested a plaque, with postage stamps honoring prominent African-Americans, from Merit Industries of Georgetown, Texas. Adpro was to select suitable stamps and fax the name and script needed on the plaque.

The plaque displays a 15-cent stamp bearing King's likeness, and stamps depicting three other famous African-Americans: Harriet Tubman, Carter G. Woodson and Paul Laurence Dunbar.

"When the package arrived, I looked at that plaque and felt an immediate chill," said Adpro owner Gerald Wilcox.

"I don't know how they can confuse a famous actor, with such a unique voice, with the man who killed a hero.

"I know there was no error from our company. We read through the order forms to be sure."

Reached in Texas, Merit's owner Herbert Miller called the mistake "a copy error" and accused Wilcox of making a mountain out of a molehill.

Miller explained, "We have a lot of girls who don't speak English, and one of them — who doesn't know James Earl Jones from a man on the moon — accidentally typed James Earl Ray."

Miller offered to correct the error, but Wilcox said that because of time, "The damage will be corrected locally."

Jones will be speaking to the Boys and Girls Club at 1 p.m. Saturday and at a reception that evening at the Inverrary Country Club.

New York Post, Sunday, November 24, 2002

nypost.com

12

BLASTER OF HIS DOMAIN

Lawrence Schwartzwald

Doug Kuntz

THEN

Billy Joel sold this luxurious Hamptons estate to TV funnyman Jerry Seinfeld in 2001 for a stunning $32 million.

NOW

Seinfeld has leveled all but 15 percent of the South Fork property without the required building permits in a multimillion-dollar renovation.

DMI

Jerry trashes Piano Man's $32M ex-home in makeover

By CLEMENTE LISI

The extensive work being done on Jerry Seinfeld's sprawling East Hampton estate is no laughing matter.

Town officials said the TV funnyman is ignoring the law because he doesn't have the proper permits to complete renovations on the posh 10½-acre home he bought from singer Billy Joel two years ago.

Seinfeld has torn down large portions of the existing mansion, which the Piano Man and his then-wife Christie Brinkley built in the 1980s.

But East Hampton officials said that 15 percent of the original house is still standing and that "a good portion" of it has illegally been removed.

Seinfeld, who shattered real-estate records when he bought the ritzy South Fork home in July 2000

for a whopping $32 million, was just supposed to replace some rotting wood on a sun porch, a terrace and a roof deck at a cost of $250,000.

But Seinfeld has redone most of the main house — of which only the original dining-room area and library remain — to include seven bedrooms, a playroom, a nursery, a dressing room and a den.

"They really shouldn't have gone that far," Tom

Preiato, who recently inspected the house, told the East Hampton Star.

The oceanfront estate also includes a three-bedroom home, a five-bedroom guest cottage and a 22-car garage.

Seinfeld has even joked that the pool in his backyard is so large, he practices kayaking in it.

Officials said the comedian's permit only allow for two small additions to the first and second

floors and that Seinfeld must get the necessary permits before they can issue him a certificate of occupancy.

Seinfeld's publicist said the comedian has not broken any laws and that he doesn't want to ruffle any feathers.

"He's not looking to create any problems with the city of East Hampton," she said. "He's a happy resident and hopes to live there indefinitely."

Grisly slay and suicide stun NYU colleagues

By JENNIFER GOULD

She was a beautiful dentist from a close family of strivers. He was a cheery secretary at the New York University clinic where she taught.

One week ago, she was found dead on the floor of her New Rochelle bedroom from multiple stab wounds to her stomach, chest and arm. He was on the bed a few feet away, with a single knife wound to the chest.

There was no sign of forced entry to her apartment, but there were signs of a struggle in the bedroom, including an overturned clock on the floor.

Next to the bed were two kitchen knives.

Described as a murder-suicide by their colleagues and families, the tragic deaths were the talk of NYU's dentistry school, where Ghada Kharouba, 37, taught clinical dentistry for the past six years and Franklin Perez, 31, worked as a receptionist.

Cops says Perez killed Kharouba and then himself. They initially referred to the two as a couple, but friends say he may have been stalking her.

"It's a tragedy for both families and everyone who knew them," said Dr. Warren Scherer, an associate division head chairman of General Dentistry at NYU.

Kharouba and her four siblings were a close, loving immigrant family who lived the American Dream.

"She was a beautiful person," said Rawya Baskaroun, a cardiologist who worked in the building. Friends of Perez describe him as a warm, caring friend.

Victoria's knickers in a million $ knot

Victoria's Secret Stores Inc. has agreed to pay $4.25 million to settle a class-action lawsuit brought by California store managers who claimed the lingerie retailer failed to pay them for doing extra work.

The settlement, reached last month with the help of a mediator, was approved Thursday by a judge.

The lawsuit claimed the Ohio-based company had a corporate practice of authorizing inadequate staffing levels that placed customer service and non-management duties onto managers. *AP*

24
nypost.com
New York Post, Sunday, June 15, 2003

Dealers stash coke to keep supplies up

By SAM SMITH

Local dealers are stockpiling tons of cocaine in anticipation of a shortage sparked by recent gains in the global war on the drug, The Post has learned.

But the stockpile is so vast, drug cops say, it could be up to a year before any change is detected on New York streets.

Thanks to U.S.-funded eradication efforts, cocaine production in Colombia is waning, according to a recent U.N. report.

The latest strike against Colombian growing operations came after even greater successes against drug lords in Peru and Bolivia, according to the Drug Enforcement Administration.

"We have a full-court press on all three [sources of cocaine]," said Anthony Placido, the DEA's special agent in charge of the New York field division.

"Now we've got a shot at making a meaningful impact."

But Placido says he's not "overly optimistic" that the impact of the recent successes at source level will flow quickly down to the street.

Ar-rib-ederci, Roma

Famed restaurateur Tony is dead at 78

LOS ANGELES — Tony Roma, whose casual rib joint became an international restaurant empire after it caught the attention of a Texas financier in the 1970s, died Friday of lung cancer at a hospice. He was 78.

Roma opened his first barbecue restaurant in north Miami in the early 1970s, according to his company's Web site.

The restaurant originally specialized in steaks and burgers, but that changed when Roma and his chef decided to offer barbecued ribs as a weekend special.

The ribs proved so popular that they came to dominate the menu, and Roma's restaurants opened across the United States, in Japan, England and Canada.

While once popular in the New York area, Tony Roma's no longer has a presence here. A search of the company's Web site indicates the chain's nearest eateries are in Maryland.

The company went international after the late Texas financier and Dallas Cowboys owner Clint Murchison Jr. visited Miami for the 1976 Super Bowl and stopped at Roma's restaurant.

He enjoyed the food so much, he bought the majority U.S. franchise rights from Roma and established a jointly owned company.

The restaurants expanded rapidly through the 1980s and now number more than 250.

The chain officially celebrated its 30th anniversary last year.

In early 1982, Roma was in the news for his engagement to blond bombshell actress Stella Stevens. The engagement, announced in April, was off and on again until it was officially broken in June.

Roma lived in Palm Springs, Calif., but moved to the hospice in Hemet, 90 miles southeast of Los Angeles, about 10 days ago, said Faye Otto, the hospice owner.   AP

HOT & SPICY: Tony Roma, here at one of his Florida outlets, built his chain into 250 restaurants.   *AP*

Dubya due in Apple on fund tour

WASHINGTON — President Bush begins raising money in earnest this week for his 2004 re-election effort with a two-week, cross-country sprint that brings him to the Big Apple next week and is expected to take in millions of dollars.

First lady Laura Bush and the president's 2004 running mate, Vice President Dick Cheney, also will hit the fund-raising circuit.

In all, the president is expected to raise $200 million or more for his primary campaign over the next several months, at least twice the record $100 million he collected for the 2000 primaries.

Helping Bush are fund-raising volunteers, including the "Pioneers" who played a key role in 2000 by raising at least $100,000 each. A new class of fund-raisers, known as the "Rangers," will collect at least $200,000 each for Bush's campaign.

He plans his first fund-raiser Tuesday in Washington, followed by a series of $2,000-per-person events, including a June 23 gathering in New York.

AP

Post Weather Report

For current forecasts go to: **NYPOST.com**

Sunday

Today: Mostly sunny; warm and less humid. High 80 to 84.

Tonight: Mainly clear. Low 60 to 64

Monday

Tomorrow: Sunny and pleasant. High 72 to 76.

Tomorrow night: Mainly clear. Low 58 to 62

Tuesday

Mostly sunny. High 76 to 80.

Evening Clear. Low 62 to 66

Wednesday

Clouds, sun. High 78 to 82.

Evening P/cloudy. Low 64 to 68

Almanac

YESTERDAY'S CONDITIONS AT CENTRAL PARK
Temperature
High: 81, Low: 59, Mean: 70
Departure from Normal
Yesterday: -1 degrees
Precipitation
Yesterday: 0.01", Month: 6.66", Year: 24.72", Normal year to date: 20.88"
Cooling Degree days Yesterday............5
Total for the month 30
Total since Jan. 1 51
Last year 179
Ozone reading (for Sun.) ...Not available
UV Index (for Sun.) .... 8 (High)
HEAT INDEX (at noon)
Actual air temperature was 74
Actual dew point was 68, making a heat index of 75 yesterday.
Humidity (at noon) 81%
POLLEN
High. Predominant pollen: Pine, Hickory, Pecan

Peekskill 78/55
White Plains 76/57
Stamford 77/57
Bridgeport 75/58
Sussex 76/54
Paterson 78/56
Garden City 78/59
Huntington 78/59
Riverhead 74/53
Montauk 72/54
Southhampton 74/53
Newark 78/61
La G 82/62
JFK 81/60
Deer Park 78/58
Long Beach 78/60
Sandy Hook 76/59
Asbury Park 75/58
Manasquan 74/57
Toms River 77/57
Long Beach 70/57
Atlantic City 74/57
Ocean City 74/58
CONN.
N.Y.
N.J.

Sun and Moon

Sunrise today .... 5:23 a.m.
Sunset tonight .... 8:29 p.m.
Moonrise today .... 10:17 p.m.
Moonset today .... 6:12 a.m.

Last | New | First | Full
June 21 | June 29 | July 6 | July 13

Forecast data is current as of 6 p.m. yesterday. Temperatures are today's highs and tonight's lows.

Weather (W): s-sunny, pc-partly cloudy, c-cloudy, sh-showers, r-rain, t-thunderstorms, sf-snow flurries, sn-snow, I-ice

Sunday, June 15, 2003

Seattle 72/50
Billings 81/56
Minneapolis 84/62
Detroit 80/58
New York 82/62
San Francisco 70/56
Chicago 76/55
Washington 80/64
PLEASANT
Denver 85/59
Kansas City 84/62
Los Angeles 79/64
El Paso 92/66
Houston 88/72
Atlanta 85/69
HUMID
Miami 88/78

Showers
T-storms
Rain
Flurries
Snow
Ice

Shown are noon positions of weather systems and precipitation. Temperature bands are highs for the day. Forecast high/low temperatures are given for selected cities.

Fronts
Cold
Warm
Stationary

All forecasts and maps provided by AccuWeather, Inc. ©2003

New York Tides

High Tide for	TODAY 1st	2nd	TOMORROW 1st	2nd
Coney Island	9:12a	9:31p	10:07a	10:24p
Fire Island	8:36a	8:55p	9:31a	9:48p
Hempstead	9:34a	9:53p	10:29a	10:46p
Huntington	12:08a	12:45p	1:00a	1:38p
Jones Inlet	8:56a	9:15p	9:51a	10:08p
Montauk Point	10:09a	10:36p	11:04a	11:30p
Port Washington	12:13a	1:01p	1:09a	1:57p
Sandy Hook	9:16a	9:35p	10:11a	10:28p

Regional cities

	TODAY	TOMORROW
Albany	78/52/s	77/53/s
Danbury	78/52/s	69/49/pc
Glens Falls	78/49/s	76/51/s
Gr Barrington	77/48/s	72/48/s
Kingston	78/52/s	74/51/pc
Liberty	78/49/s	72/51/pc
Monticello	78/49/s	72/51/pc
Newburgh	78/54/s	74/52/pc
Poughkeepsie	78/52/s	74/51/pc
Saratoga Springs	78/51/s	77/52/s
Stroudsburg	78/57/pc	72/55/s
Torrington	78/51/s	71/49/s
Syracuse	76/52/s	77/55/s

World cities

	TODAY	TOMORROW
Amsterdam	68/58/pc	69/60/pc
Athens	92/73/s	90/71/pc
Beijing	87/66/s	89/73/s
Berlin	74/55/pc	75/56/pc
Cairo	100/69/s	103/70/s
Dublin	67/52/pc	68/47/pc
Geneva	84/60/pc	83/62/pc
Helsinki	55/34/c	55/39/c
Hong Kong	81/76/t	82/75/r
Jerusalem	86/59/s	88/61/s
London	76/60/pc	79/61/s
Madrid	92/64/pc	93/62/pc
Mexico City	81/57/pc	77/51/r
Montreal	71/51/pc	67/53/pc
Moscow	62/39/pc	60/38/c
Paris	81/61/s	78/60/s
Rio de Janeiro	79/65/pc	79/67/pc
Rome	94/72/pc	92/71/pc
Sydney	58/40/s	62/43/s
Tokyo	75/66/t	76/70/r

WAKSAL THE FLOORS

Sad Sam will work in Pa. prison

EXCLUSIVE

By AL GUART
and JOHN LEHMANN

Martha Stewart's champagne-swilling, insider-trading pal, Sam Waksal, will do his time in a prison facility in the mountains of Pennsylvania where he'll be working for as little as 16 cents an hour cleaning dishes and sweeping floors.

The disgraced ImClone founder wanted the Bureau of Prisons to find him a spot in balmy Florida at Eglin Air Force Base — a facility once rated by Forbes magazine as the "Best Place to be Incarcerated" in America.

But The Post learned yesterday the disgraced biotech entrepreneur has been told to surrender at the Schuylkill Federal Correctional Institute in Minersville, Pa.

While Waksal will be housed in Schuylkill's minimum-security facility, his new life will have little in common with his high-flying days on the Manhattan celebrity cocktail circuit.

He'll be put to work from 7:30 a.m. to 3:30 p.m. five days a week, undertaking menial tasks, such as cleaning cooking utensils, trimming garden beds and sweeping floors, prison sources said.

Instead of pulling in millions of dollars a year, he'll be working for between 16 cents and 40 cents an hour.

About 300 inmates are housed in the camp facility, sleeping in dormitory-style accommodations and sharing a TV room, Bureau of Prisons spokesman Dan Dunne said.

Internet access is forbidden.

"Schuylkill's not the worst place to be, but it's certainly not as nice as Eglin and it's going to get cold up there in winter," said

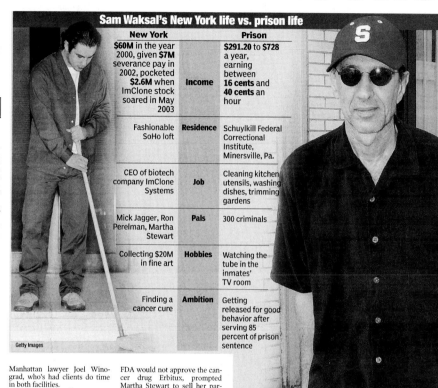

Sam Waksal's New York life vs. prison life

	New York		Prison
Income	$60M in the year 2000, given $7M severance pay in 2002, pocketed $2.6M when ImClone stock soared in May 2003		$291.20 to $728 a year, earning between 16 cents and 40 cents an hour
Residence	Fashionable SoHo loft		Schuylkill Federal Correctional Institute, Minersville, Pa.
Job	CEO of biotech company ImClone Systems		Cleaning kitchen utensils, washing dishes, trimming gardens
Pals	Mick Jagger, Ron Perelman, Martha Stewart		300 criminals
Hobbies	Collecting $20M in fine art		Watching the tube in the inmates' TV room
Ambition	Finding a cancer cure		Getting released for good behavior after serving 85 percent of prison sentence

Getty Images

Waksal visits his sick mother on July 4, when he was granted a one-day release.

Robert Kalfus

Manhattan lawyer Joel Winograd, who's had clients do time in both facilities.

"It looks like a college campus — there's no gates or fences."

Waksal, 55, is due to begin serving his seven-year, three-month sentence on July 23. Manhattan federal Judge William Pauley handed down the stiff sentence after Waksal pleaded guilty to eight federal charges, including securities fraud, conspiracy, obstruction of justice, perjury and bank fraud.

Waksal's sudden attempts to dump more than $10 million in family-held ImClone shares on Dec. 27, 2001 after learning the

FDA would not approve the cancer drug Erbitux, prompted Martha Stewart to sell her parcel of nearly 4,000 shares, the feds charge.

Stewart has been given a new court date of July 21 for arguments to be heard on motions filed by her legal team.

The motions, which are being kept confidential by Judge Miriam Goldman Cedarbaum, tackle several matters, including the grand jury which indicted Stewart last month on securities fraud, conspiracy and lying to a federal agent.

She is due to face trial Jan. 12.

Spurned lady cop 'a suicide'

By MURRAY WEISS
and KIERAN CROWLEY

The female NYPD lieutenant found shot dead in her Nassau home was romantically involved with a married cop, and investigators speculate she may have killed herself because he would not leave his wife, law enforcement sources said.

The gun found next to Lt. Theresa Flannery's body Wednesday morning was hers and had been fired three times, the sources said.

Long Island cops believe she missed her first shot and fired a second time, hitting herself in the face. Bleeding and in pain,

she put the gun behind her ear and pulled the trigger yet again, striking herself in the back of the head, sources said.

Flannery, 33, a 12-year-veteran, was on the list to become a captain. Police Commissioner Ray Kelly yesterday described her as a "very well-respected officer."

An autopsy was completed, but pending further testing, her death was not classified as either a suicide or a homicide.

Law enforcement sources said that Flannery left her husband, also an NYPD lieutenant, when she started seeing her cop boyfriend. She was upset because he was not yet willing to leave his wife for her, the sources said.

Princess Di comic gets throne away

Now she'll have to un-Di another day.

Marvel Comics has scrapped its plan to resurrect Princess Diana as a mutant superhero in the pages of its "X-Men" spin-off, "X-Statix."

The storyline was to be called "Di Another Day."

Marvel said, "While Lady Diana was portrayed in a positive light in the comic book, upon reflection, the company has decided to remove Princess Diana and all references to the royal family."

Dareh Gregorian

Rage 'urns' hubby harass rap

By PHILIP MESSING

A Staten Island man capped a fight with his wife by smashing the urn that held her late mother's ashes, police said yesterday.

Dwight Johnson, 38, went into a rage last month at the home of his estranged wife, Vanessa, 36, on Gordon Street, in the Stapleton section of Staten Island, police said.

At 5 a.m. on June 8, he allegedly took a knife to a couch and chair before he smashed several dishes, a TV set, and a wall unit.

The violent outburst caused an urn containing the ashes of Vanessa's late mother to go careening to the ground and shatter into many pieces, spreading her remains all over the living

room floor and into adjoining areas of the house, police said.

Johnson followed up his tirade with another stunt on Monday, police said.

From 2 to 9 p.m., Johnson allegedly peppered his wife with more than 20 phone calls, saying, "Tell those damn cops to stop going to my mother's house," according to a criminal complaint obtained by The Post.

Johnson, who has been married to Vanessa for about three years, was arrested at his mother's residence in East New York on Wednesday afternoon.

He was charged with criminal mischief and aggravated harassment for the June incident and the Monday phone call barrage.

★★

3

New York Post, Sunday, December 14, 2003

nypost.com

JIGGLE ALL THE WAY

Boob jobs, lipo in Santa's bag

SWELL GIFT: Dana Caruso is two bra sizes bigger thanks to the Christmas spirit of hubby Al. N.Y. Post: Jim Alcorn

By SUSAN EDELMAN

All I want for Christmas is my two new breasts.

That's the jingle many women are singing this year as breast augmentation and other cosmetic surgeries grow in popularity as holiday gifts.

"You're always searching for that perfect thing you think someone wants. He knew what I wanted — there was no guesswork involved," said Dana Caruso, 35, a mother of two whose husband, Al, bought her a $7,000 breast job for Christmas.

Giving "the gift of beauty" is booming, said Dr. Steven Greenberg, the plastic surgeon who crafted Caruso's chest — which swelled from 36A to 36C.

"Instead of a new watch, a piece of jewelry or a vacation, they're getting a procedure they've always wanted, and it's a gift as well," he said.

Nearly 7 million Americans had cosmetic plastic surgery last year, down 12 percent from the previous year, according to the American Society of Plastic Surgeons. But more people are boldly open about doing it — and eager to do it for others, Greenberg said.

Last week, Greenberg performed liposuction on a mother of three, trimming love handles and fat from her belly and hips. Her husband paid for the $6,000 operation as a holiday gift.

"That's very common," he said.

Others buy $7,000 nose jobs for teenage or adult kids, he said. One couple recently bestowed breast implants on their college-student daughter who had always been unhappy with her bosom, Greenberg said.

Tummy tucks at $8,000 apiece and Botox and collagen injections to erase forehead wrinkles and laugh lines are also popular presents. The procedures are not covered by health insurance.

Before performing the operations, Greenberg said, he arranges a consultation with patients to make sure they are physically — and mentally — fit for the makeover.

He said he has turned away some potential patients with "unrealistic expectations," like a 180-pounder who wants to look like Britney Spears.

Caruso, who runs a beauty institute in Levittown, said she had yearned for a bigger bust since adolescence — and never kept her desire a secret from her husband.

A few months ago, he raised the touchy subject.

"You've always wanted it," Caruso's husband told her. "I think it would be a really nice Christmas gift. How do you feel about it?"

She said yes without hesitation. Caruso, who went under the knife five weeks ago, described the results as "fabulous" — though she's no Pamela Anderson.

"Oh my God, it looks so natural. You couldn't tell I had the surgery," she said.

Caruso can't thank her husband enough for the Christmas cleavage.

"It's something I've wanted for so long," she said.

Snow to give us sopping days before Christmas

By ALISHA BERGER and BRIDGET HARRISON

Cancel the Christmas shopping — it's snow time again!

Just as New York has shaken off last week's icy slush, a nasty new nor'easter will hit today, pounding the city with more snow and heavy rain.

The wintry storm is set to dump 2 to 4 inches of snow on the city in the morning before temperatures rise a little, turning the white stuff into torrential rain this afternoon and tonight.

And while it comes down

in buckets on New York, regions north of the city may get as much as 6 to 10 inches of snow.

Areas including Passaic and Bergen counties in New Jersey, and Westchester, Rockland and Orange counties and other parts of the lower Hudson Valley will likely take the brunt and are on winter storm watch.

The conditions will make shopping miserable on this second-to-last weekend before Christmas.

"If it's a blizzard like they anticipate, we're staying home," said Claribel Vargas, 36, of The Bronx, who was

trying to get through her holiday shopping checklist.

John and Laura Scott, who drove to the city from Baltimore for the weekend, said they weren't looking forward to leaping over

flooded crosswalks.

"We heard it was going to snow, but we're going to keep going," said Laura Scott, 32.

Cyndy Patton, 46, from Erie, Pa., in town for the

weekend with her daughter, said she knew about the snow but came anyway.

"We've braved rain and snowstorms before. We book it, we come," she said.

But respite is around the corner. The rain will taper off, replaced by two tranquil days with temperatures reaching the 40s. But beware, another nor'easter will hit the city on Wednesday or Thursday, says the National Weather Service.

Weather forecast / Page 26

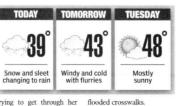

TODAY	TOMORROW	TUESDAY
39°	43°	48°
Snow and sleet changing to rain	Windy and cold with flurries	Mostly sunny

Wassail the fuss about this feat?

A cheery crowd of 519 Christmas carolers braved the New York cold and fa-la-la-la'd themselves into the Guinness Book of World Records yesterday with the largest carol service, breaking the previous record of 517.

"My fingers froze but, hey, we broke the record," said Norman Ellis who joined the sing-along on the steps of the General Post Office across from Madison Square Garden.

Twelve Guinness marshals confirmed carolers were singing and not just moving their lips. *Reuters*

26

New York Post, Thursday, April 7, 2005

nypost.com

Elevator moo goo guy ran

Hides from immigration

By LUKAS I. ALPERT
and JOHN DOYLE

The Chinese food deliver-yman who was trapped for 3½ days in an elevator went into hiding yesterday — fearing his newfound fame may get him in hot-and-sour soup with immigration officials.

"He left the city," one of Ming Kuang Chen's room-mates said through an inter-preter. "He's an illegal im-migrant and he's afraid people will catch him."

After his ordeal — which set off an intensive police manhunt — Chen's co-workers at the Happy Dra-gon restaurant in The Bronx said they didn't know if he would return to work.

"He's recovering. We don't know if he's coming back. We haven't spoken to him," said a woman work-ing the counter.

Immigration officials, however, say Chen has little to worry about despite his picture being splashed all over the news.

"If the guy doesn't come up as a major hit, like a na-tional security threat or with a violent criminal re-cord we just don't have the resources to pursue every single case," said an official who spoke on condition an-onymity. "He's a nobody."

Regardless, Mayor Bloom-berg is furious that Chen's immigration status was re-vealed as cops searched for him.

"It's unconscionable. His immigration status had nothing to do with it what-soever. It should not have been divulged," he said yes-terday. "It would be in di-rect violations of the execu-tive order that I signed."

MING KUANG CHEN
"He left the city."

In 2003, Bloomberg strengthened a longstanding rule that prevented city em-ployees, such as police offi-cers or social service work-ers, from reporting the immigration status of resi-dents to Immigration and Customs Enforcement.

Chen says he got stuck in the elevator Friday evening after making several deliv-eries in the Tracey Towers on West Mosholu Parkway South. He remained there — caught between floors — until Tuesday morning.

Chen insists he repeatedly pressed the elevator's alarm and intercom but could not communicate his situation to building employees be-cause he speaks little Eng-lish. The building's manag-ers, however, say they didn't hear a thing from Chen until Tuesday.

Meanwhile, after he didn't return to work, Chen's em-ployers called police who launched a full-on manhunt, going door to door in the building and searching sur-rounding parks with blood-hounds. Little did they know, Chen was in their midst the whole time.

Bailed mobster busted again

A suspected Genovese family associate — who was free on bail pending trial in an alleged horse-doping and illegal sports-betting ring — was busted again yesterday for try-ing to extort gambling customers, authorities said.

Emilio Testa, 39, was charged in January with conducting an illegal gambling business and gambling conspiracy. But after he posted bail, he allegedly set up new sports betting accounts.

One of his customers became a federal informant, and Testa is caught on tape threatening him over a $250,000 debt, authorities said.
Carl Campanile

Warm spirit of 75

CONEY STYLIN': Boardwalk babes Erika Cifuentes (left) and Silvia Ogonaga heat up a Coney Island calendar shoot by Rob Lang yesterday.

City basks in year's best weather

By JEN KELLY

It officially began 2½ weeks ago, but spring fi-nally hit New York yester-day when the temperature topped 70 degrees for the first time since October — and kept on rising to a balmy 75.

Sun-starved New York-ers ditched their coats and scarves in favor of sun-glasses and short sleeves as thousands jammed into parks to enjoy lunch, ham-mer at their laptops or soak up some rays.

In Coney Island, fashion photographer Rob Lang

took advantage of the sunny day to trot out some beach beauties onto the boardwalk in a shoot for an upcoming calendar.

Manhattan lawyer Bill Kracklauer, 42, made the most of the bright sun-shine at Bryant Park to enjoy a rare pleasure — a cigar. "It wasn't that bad a winter — but it just never went away," he said.

National Weather Serv-ice forecaster Michael Silva said the temperature reached 70 at about 2 p.m. yesterday at Central Park and topped at 75 at 3:05 p.m.

"Normal for this time of year is 57, so we're well above normal," he said.

The NWS is predicting a high of 70 degrees today — but also a chance of thunderstorms this after-noon.

Tomorrow will bring a chance of rain, and a pre-dicted high in the mid-50s.

The weekend is ex-pected to be mostly sunny, with a high of around 60 both days.

**Weather report /
Page 32**

ANGELA HILL
In tears on witness stand.

'Rough sex' is defense in kidnap

By LAURA ITALIANO

The "rough sex" defense reared its ugly head in a Manhattan courtroom yes-terday, on Day Two of an already-ugly kidnap trial.

Jurors listened intently as the lawyer for the defen-dant — aspiring soap-opera actor Carlos Leiva — grilled his accuser.

Leiva, 41, allegedly went into a jealous rage in March 2004 against his girlfriend, Angela Hill. The model had spent Tuesday on the stand describing her six-hour or-deal, during which Leiva al-legedly held her at knife point, forced her to strip and beat her.

But defense lawyer Jo-seph Corozzo used his questioning to imply that the accuser — Angela Hill, 28 — had violent propensi-ties of her own. She liked it rough, he insinuated, in a line of questioning so force-ful, it at times reduced the woman to tears.

Corozzo tried, and failed, to get Hill to admit that hours before the incident, she was dancing on a bar-stool at the nightclub Lobby and got into a fight with the woman. He did get Hill to admit to pleading guilty in 1996 to hurling a fire extinguisher at her then-beau.

Then, the lawyer raised the "rough sex" defense — implying that at least some of Hill's bruises came dur-ing consensual sex. "Did you have sex on the hard wood floors at all that night?" he asked. The ques-tion was disallowed.

Booze bad for new moms' milk

Drinking even small amounts of alcohol cuts the amount of milk new moms produce and adversely af-fects breast-feeding, a new study reveals.

Researchers found that just one or two glasses of wine negatively affected the hormones responsible for milk production.

The research is published in The Journal of Clinical Endocrinology and Metabo-lism. *Bill Hoffmann*

New York Post, Friday, September 16, 2005   nypost.com   7

'Shoot me' man's ma hails cops

By JOHN DOYLE

The mother of the ax-wielding Brooklyn man police shot in the stomach said her son is "all messed up" — and she doesn't blame the cop who shot him.

Debra Wilson, 47, yesterday told The Post police were justified in shooting her son, Alfonso, once in the stomach after he refused to drop the ax, telling police they'd have to shoot him first.

"I don't blame the police, because [the officer] did what he had to do; my son had a weapon.

"He really needs help, he really does. They shouldn't just lock him up — he needs psychiatric help."

Wilson said her son "got an attitude" while she and boyfriend Derek Coleman were talking to her 21-year-old son about an unpaid $280 phone bill about 7 p.m. Wednesday.

"It was just a conversation," Wilson said. "We were discussing it with him and he got an attitude.

"He's not right in the head — his head is all messed up."

When Coleman threw Alfonso out of the apartment on Ocean Avenue in Flatbush, the enraged son went to the boiler room, came back with a fire ax and took several swings at the door, putting four deep scars in the wood.

Alfonso was still wielding the ax when police arrived and shouted at him to drop it, but had to shoot him when he issued his challenge.

Alfonso was in stable condition yesterday at Kings County Hospital.

DA puts byte on 'kid porn' teach

A high-school teacher's home computer contained more than 1,000 files of kiddie porn, including images of infants, when it was seized during his arrest, police said yesterday.

"This is sick stuff," said a law-enforcement source.

Cops found the pictures after raiding the Brooklyn apartment of Madison HS English teacher Craig Roffman, who was arraigned yesterday in Brooklyn on 187 counts of possessing child porn.

He was fired from the school shortly after the July raid.

Cops said they moved in on Roffman after Florida police arrested a man whose AOL screen name was "Jupiter Perv."

Police found 11 e-mails from Roffman to Jupiter Perv containing child porn, leading them to the cache in the computer. Roffman was freed on $16,000 bail yesterday.   *Jim Hinch*

PLAGUE ON YOUR MOUSES

Corbis

Jeremy Sprig

EEK! Three mice carrying plague are missing from the Public Health Research Institute (left), where scientists are working on a vaccine.

Tiny killer

■ People usually get the plague from being bitten by a rodent flea that is carrying the plague bacterium or by handling an infected animal.

■ Plague is an infectious disease of animals and humans caused by a bacterium named *Yersinia pestis*.

■ Modern antibiotics are effective against plague, but if an infected person is not treated promptly, the disease is likely to cause illness or death.

■ About 14 percent (1 in 7) of all plague cases in the United States are fatal.

■ Plague in the United States has occurred as mostly scattered cases in rural areas (an average of 10 to 15 persons each year). Globally, the World Health Organization reports 1,000 to 3,000 cases of plague every year.

Source: Centers for Disease Control

Bubonic-infected critters vanish from bio-terror lab in Newark

By LEONARD GREENE

The cat must have been away.

New Jersey health officials have no other explanation for why three mice carrying the devastating bubonic plague are missing from separate cages at a bio-terror research facility in Newark.

The FBI has agents scurrying for clues — and the Centers for Disease Control and the University of Medicine and Dentistry of New Jersey have launched investigations into why a top-level bio-containment lab is unable to locate rodents used in ex-

periments on the deadly plague.

Scientists are trying to find new vaccinations for the disease, which federal officials fear could be used as a biological weapon.

Doctors at the Public Health Research Institute, which leases space from the Newark campus, were unavailable for comment, but the brownish-gray critters were reported missing Aug. 29 after a vaccination experiment.

Workers at the lab called the CDC and the FBI immediately, officials said.

The FBI responded with members of its Joint

Terrorism Task Force and experts in biological agents that are used to create biological weapons.

Administrators at the research institute blame either theft or an accounting error. The missing mice could have also been eaten by others used in the experiment, they said.

No one will ever know, they said, because the cages that held the mice were sterilized and incinerated, eliminating any evidence.

"We're trying to understand what occurred," said CDC spokesman Von Roebuck. "It looks like there's no indication

that there is any public health threat. We've had no reports of plague in the area."

Investigators still interrogated about two dozen employees and lab researchers, some of whom were given lie detector tests, officials said.

Doctors at the lab injected the mice with the bacterium Yersinia pestis, which causes bubonic and other forms of plague. Some mice were given a proven vaccine, some were given an experimental vaccine and some were given no vaccine at all.

Researchers said infected mice usually die quickly, reducing the risk to humans.

People usually get the plague from being bitten by a rodent flea that is carrying the plague bacterium or by handling an infected animal, according to the CDC.

Throughout history, the infectious plague has killed more than 30 million people, including one-third of Europe during the Black Death of the 1300s.

The last urban plague epidemic occurred in Los Angeles in 1924-25.

Modern antibiotics can treat the disease if it is diagnosed quickly, but even medical experts still shake at the mention of its name.

New York Post, Wednesday, November 15, 2006   nypost.com

3

WHEN YOU GOTTA GOYA, YOU GOTTA GOYA

Bandits grab art as movers make 'P' stop

By MARSHA KRANES

A simple pit stop by the side of the highway led to the theft of an priceless painting by Spanish master Francisco de Goya while it was being transported to New York from Ohio for an exhibit at the Guggenheim Museum.

The 1778 masterpiece, "Children With a Cart," was snatched when the professional art movers took a break on the side of the highway en route to the Big Apple and left their vehicle — and the nearly 5-foot-by-3-foot painting — unattended, said FBI spokeswoman Jerri Williams.

When they returned to their vehicle, the movers discovered it had been broken into and the painting had been swiped, she said.

It was the only artwork they were transporting — and that makes investigators believe the thieves didn't just chance upon the masterpiece.

"It's highly likely they knew what they were taking. It appears they knew what they were doing," said Williams.

The spokeswoman said the theft happened when the movers were parked near an interstate highway outside Scranton, Pa., but she would not reveal whether it was at a rest stop or restaurant. She also would not identify the transporter or the type of vehicle they were driving.

"We're conducting a full investigation but we have no reason to believe at this time that anybody involved with the painting's transport was involved with the plot," Williams said.

The theft took place Nov. 7 but wasn't disclosed until late Monday in a joint statement issued by the Guggenheim and the Goya's owner, the Toledo Museum of Art.

They said the painting was insured for just over $1 million, which art experts described as "on the low side."

This heist was not the first time the Spanish masterpiece was stolen.

Guy Wildenstein, president of Wildenstein & Co., which sold the Goya to the Toledo museum, said the painting was ripped off in 1869 when it was hanging in the Royal Palace of El Prado, in Madrid, Spain. He didn't know how or when it was recovered.

"I think [the stolen Goya] would be quite impossible to sell," said Wildenstein. "The museums have photos of it, pictures of it are being circulated through newspapers. It will be very difficult for anyone to resell this painting."

Asked whom would have stolen it — and

ARTFUL HEIST: Goya's "Children With a Cart" was lifted from a truck bringing it to New York for an exhibit at the Guggenheim.

why — if it couldn't be resold, he said "Maybe somebody who's looking to collect a ransom and give back the picture. I don't see any other monetary value to the painting to anyone."

The artwork, which the Toledo museum purchased in 1959, was on loan to the Guggenheim for its upcoming exhibit, "Spanish Painting from El Greco to Picasso: Time, Truth and History."

The exhibit is slated to open Friday. The insurers are offering a $50,000 reward for information leading to its recovery.

Meanwhile, two Renaissance paintings missing for more than 200 years were discovered hanging in the study of a librarian in London, and will be auctioned by the woman's heirs.

The librarian, Jean Preston, bought the two works by Fra Angelico in California

in the 1960s for about $380.

An art historian learned that the two had been among a set of six small panels depicting saints that were scattered when Napoleon invaded Italy in the 1790s.

Preston, a retired curator of manuscripts at Princeton University, died earlier this year.

With Post Wire Services

marsha.kranes@nypost.com

New York Post, Wednesday, December 13, 2006   nypost.com

17 to life in Queens daddy slay

A man was sentenced to 17 years to life in prison yesterday for killing his roommate in front of the victim's horrified young daughter.

Ricardo "Teddy" Lyons, 27, who lived on the lam for years in Ohio, was convicted in Queens in October thanks to the testimony of Summer Peynado, who was just 7 when she saw Lyons hold down her dad while another man shot him in the head.

Summer had been visiting her father, Nicholas Peynado, 46, that day in June 2002.

Peynado shared the Jamaica house with Lyons and a third man, Dwayne Wright, and the three got into an argument.

Summer, now 12, testified about hearing the loud "pop" of a gun as the men argued.

She said she then witnessed her father being dragged outside and watched through the window as Wright shot him execution-style while Lyons held him down.

Wright, who ran away with Lyons, has yet to be captured.

Ikimulisa Livingston

Hope for N.Y. climber

Rescuers got two breaks yesterday in the three-day race to find a Brooklyn climber and two pals stranded on Oregon's Mount Hood — clearer skies and a more precise location of one climber.

Following Monday's blizzard, searchers resumed their climb to try to find Jerry "Nikko" Cooke, 36, of Bay Ridge, and Texans Kelly James, 44, and Brian Hall, 37.

They also were able to zero in on the injured James, who called home on his cellphone Sunday. The cellphone signal allowed engineers to track his whereabouts to within 1,500 feet.

John Doyle, Post Wires

6-day deadlock for samurai jury

A weary jury entered its sixth day of deliberations yesterday in the case of a Long Island man accused of nearly decapitating his stepfather with a samurai sword, and remains deadlocked.

They are deciding the fate of Zachary Gibian, 20, who stands accused of second-degree murder in the grisly slaying of retired NYPD cop Scott Nager, 51, as he slept on a couch in their Hauppauge home in February 2005.   *Selim Algar*

Wii REGRET TO DEFORM YOU

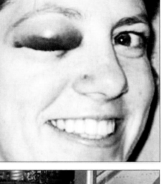

Photos: Splash News

NINTEN-WOE: A blog, WiiHaveAProblem.com, documents how Nintendo's new remote-control game wand (right) has been accidentally flung into TV sets, broken windows and even given a black eye to a player's girlfriend.

Smash vid game gives players a beating

By LEELA de KRETSER

Nintendo's latest gaming technology is causing a "Wii" problem for a growing number of excited players who have flung, swung and pitched the special controller wand into television screens, ceiling fans — and faces.

Collateral damage from the Wii Remote — a video game controller that is motion-sensitive and allows players to physically interact with the screen — is being tallied by a new Web site that keeps track of accidents caused by overzealous users losing control of their sensors.

Cracked television screens, smashed dishes, broken ceiling fans and black eyes are all documented on WiiHaveAProblem.com, a new blog dedicated to the mishaps of using the Nintendo controller to play virtual baseball, boxing and basketball in the living room.

"Unfortunately, my courage was far greater than my skill," posts a victim known as Jim, who attached a picture of his girlfriend, Liz, sporting a black eye after the latest Nintendo system was brought into their home.

"[Liz] approached me from the side, appearing from my blind spot, while I was performing a slashing movement. I hit her with full force right in her eye!" he wrote.

By far the greatest problem for users is the thin strap attached to the Wii remote breaking mid-movement.

Prompted by photo documentation supplied by Wii users on the Web, Nintendo last week reported it was investigating reports of problems with the strap that secures the remote to the wrist.

"Some people are getting a lot more excited than we'd expected," Nintendo president Satoru Iwata said.

Ohio techie Jim Walsh, who designed the Web site, told The Post he was surprised by the attention his blog had received since he launched it last month.

As a result of his postings, Walsh said Nintendo had introduced thicker straps for its launch of the Wii in Europe.

Nintendo did not return phone calls for comment.

Some of the Wii accidents re-ported by Walsh on the site are clearly caused by owner stupidity.

"Jessica" posts that she was playing baseball with her Wii when a losing streak prompted her to angrily pitch the remote control across the virtual plate.

"With all my might I promptly slammed my hand (and Wii controller) into my oak coffee table," she wrote.

"The Wii broke apart, cutting the inside of my finger."

Walsh, 27, who does not own a Wii, said he receives about 20 to 30 reports a day of broken furniture and home items, as well as injuries.

"What we're actually posting is probably only a fraction of what is going on out there," he said.

Tragic nose-job teen's ma: Sack doc

A Park Avenue plastic surgeon should be stripped of his license for allegedly botching a nose job and killing a Brooklyn College honors student, her heart-broken parents said yesterday.

"I want to stop him from working," said Tali Glisko. "He didn't even apologize once. I'm going to make sure that he's going to stop working."

She is planning to sue Dr. Yoel Shahar for the death of her daughter Mor Glisko, 18.

"We extend our condolences," said Shahar's lawyer, Douglas Nadjari. "He's a fine doctor and it's a tragedy for all concerned."

He said that, because of a likely lawsuit, he could not comment on the particulars of the case. The Mill Basin teen died on Thanksgiving, a day after undergoing rhinoplasty in Shahar's office.

The pretty brunette — who'd dreamed of being a corporate lawyer and starting a family — wanted the operation ever since a 2005 car accident left her nose crooked and bumped.

Jennifer Fermino

MOR GLISKO
Died on Thanksgiving.

CELEBRITIES

Best Sex I've Ever Had

To regular readers of Page Six, he'd always been The Donald. But when it was learned that real estate developer Donald Trump had split with his fashionista wife, Ivana, and taken up with a 27-year-old actress named Marla Maples, he became the focus of Page One for more than a week running.

One of those headlines became an instant classic—even more so for the photo than for the words. *Post* art editor Dennis Wickman, who designed the page, recalls that "without the right picture, it wouldn't have been the same thing. Not even close. That smug look on his face captured everything—Trump's attitude and the pride he must have felt."

Indeed, that's precisely why editors didn't worry that the quote was only a secondhand report from one of Maples' friends. (Marla herself later denied ever having said it—either about Trump, whom she later married and divorced, or anyone else.) Editor Jerry Nachman called it "the most libel-proof headline ever. I mean, what's Donald going to do—file a lawsuit saying he *wasn't* the best sex Marla ever had?"

Readers certainly enjoyed it—by the time Donald and Marla had moved back inside the paper's news pages, circulation was up over 150,000.

NEW YORK POST

METRO EDITION

WEDNESDAY, APRIL 25, 1990 / Cloudy, chance of rain, 60s today; cloudy, mid 50s tonight / Details, Page 2

40¢ in New York City 50¢ elsewhere

SAFE SEX

Donald and Ivana Trump are free to fool around with whoever they want — according to a contract signed by the couple and their lawyers: Page 5.

Don & Ivana sign 60-day pact to play the field

YOUR GUIDE TO BIG $$$$
12-page pullout: Page 33

JUNK BOND KING IN TEARS
Mike Milken cops plea: Page 3

Albert Ferreira / DMI

FOUNDED IN 1801 BY ALEXANDER HAMILTON

NEW YORK POST

LATE CITY FINAL

FRIDAY, APRIL 27, 1990 / ★★ R Sunny, mid 80s today; fair, low 60s tonight / Details, Page 2

40¢ in New York City 50¢ elsewhere

UNSAFE SEX

NEW YORK POST

SAFE SEX

Don & Ivana sign 60-day pact to play the field

YOUR GUIDE TO BIG $$$$

JUNK BOND KING IN TEARS

Ivana Trump yesterday canceled her 60-day pact with Donald that was revealed in Wednesday's Post (left). Ivana says the last thing she needs right now is to date other men. PAGE 7.

Ivana cancels 60-day 'play the field' pact with Don

New York Post: Robin Graubard

Two members of notorious Bronx gang "The Powerules," whose initiation rite is shooting a stranger in the leg.

BRONX GANG'S REIGN OF FEAR

Page 5

CELTICS WHIP KNICKS 116-105
SEATTLE CLOBBERS YANKS 6-2

Full details in Sports Section

Albert Ferreira / OMI

Donald and Ivana Trump head for their car after some bargain hunting at K mart. Talk about tough times! See Page 3.

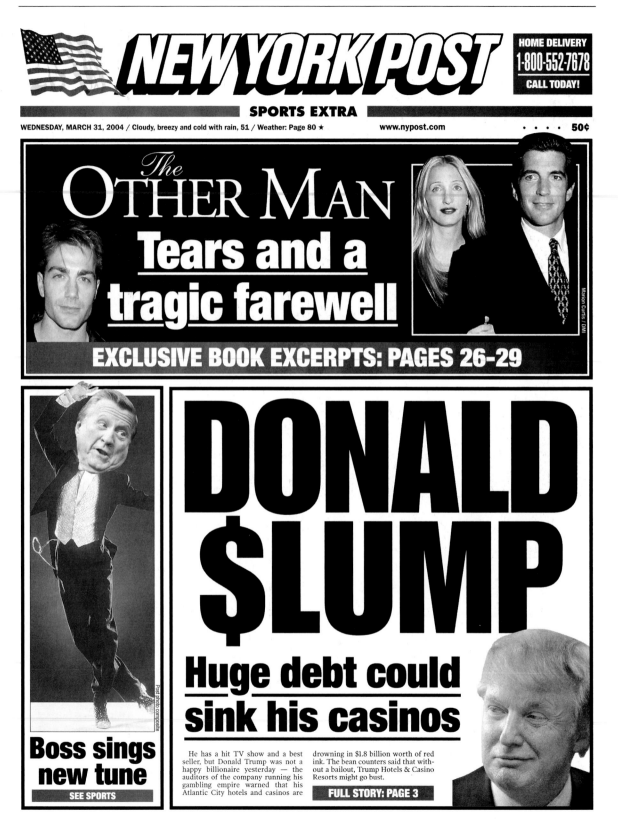

NEW YORK POST

HOME DELIVERY
1-800-552-7678
CALL TODAY!

SPORTS EXTRA

WEDNESDAY, MARCH 31, 2004 / Cloudy, breezy and cold with rain, 51 / Weather: Page 80 ★   www.nypost.com   · · · · ·   50¢

The OTHER MAN
Tears and a tragic farewell

Marion Curtis / DMI

EXCLUSIVE BOOK EXCERPTS: PAGES 26-29

Post photo composite

Boss sings new tune
SEE SPORTS

DONALD $LUMP

Huge debt could sink his casinos

He has a hit TV show and a best seller, but Donald Trump was not a happy billionaire yesterday — the auditors of the company running his gambling empire warned that his Atlantic City hotels and casinos are drowning in $1.8 billion worth of red ink. The bean counters said that without a bailout, Trump Hotels & Casino Resorts might go bust.

FULL STORY: PAGE 3

The Rev. Al Sharpton behind bars on Rikers Island yesterday.

New York Post: Ralph Ginsburg

AL-CATRAZ!

Defiant Sharpton roars from Rikers: "I'll be back louder than ever" — EXCLUSIVE INTERVIEW: Page 5

CAMP BUS TRAGEDY
Driver dies, 11 kids hurt in crash: Page 3

BUSH RIPS 'FEAR CITY'
Blasts liberals in Waldorf speech: Page 2

B'WAY STAR SHOT DEAD
Cut down by machine-gun sniper: Page 4

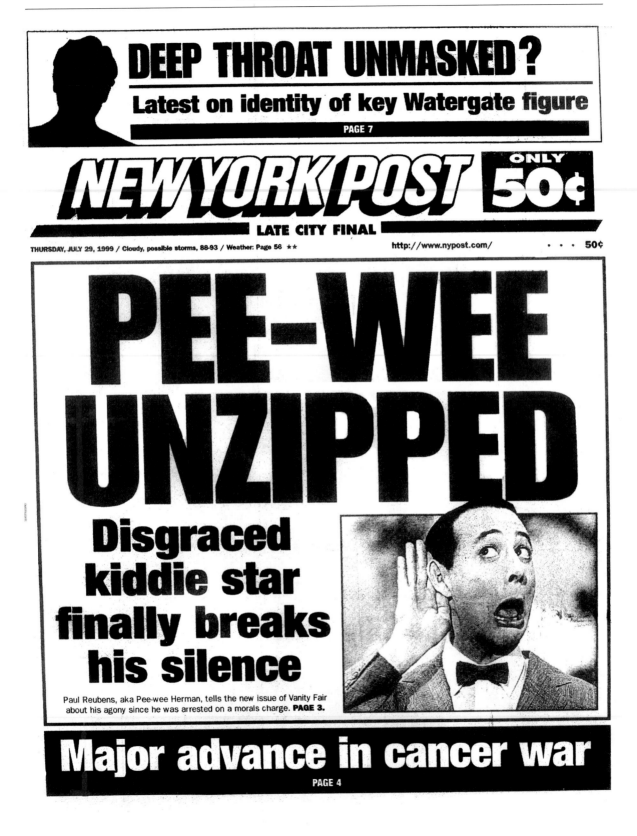

DEEP THROAT UNMASKED?

Latest on identity of key Watergate figure

PAGE 7

NEW YORK POST

ONLY 50¢

LATE CITY FINAL

THURSDAY, JULY 29, 1999 / Cloudy, possible storms, 88-93 / Weather: Page 56 ★★   http://www.nypost.com/   • • • 50¢

PEE-WEE UNZIPPED

Disgraced kiddie star finally breaks his silence

Paul Reubens, aka Pee-wee Herman, tells the new issue of Vanity Fair about his agony since he was arrested on a morals charge. **PAGE 3.**

Major advance in cancer war

PAGE 4

FOUNDED IN 1801 BY ALEXANDER HAMILTON

NEW YORK POST

LATE CITY FINAL

TUESDAY, JULY 30, 1991 / ★ ★   Rain low 70s today, cloudy chance of rain low 70s tonight. Details Page 2

40¢ New York City   50¢ elsewhere

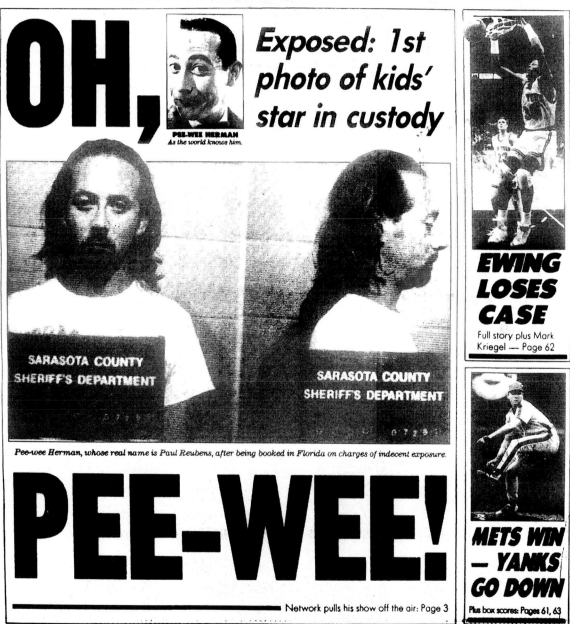

OH,

PEE-WEE HERMAN
As the world knows him.

Exposed: 1st photo of kids' star in custody

SARASOTA COUNTY SHERIFF'S DEPARTMENT

SARASOTA COUNTY SHERIFF'S DEPARTMENT

Pee-wee Herman, whose real name is Paul Reubens, after being booked in Florida on charges of indecent exposure.

PEE-WEE!

Network pulls his show off the air: Page 3

EWING LOSES CASE

Full story plus Mark Kriegel — Page 62

METS WIN — YANKS GO DOWN

Plus box scores: Pages 61, 63

FOUNDED IN 1801 BY ALEXANDER HAMILTON

NEW YORK POST

LATE CITY FINAL

FRIDAY, JULY 27, 1990 ★★ R / Cloudy, chance of rain, low 80s today; mostly cloudy, low 70s tonight / Details, Page 2   40¢ in New York City 50¢ elsewhere

Now you can call her Roseanne . . .

BARR-F!

TV star mocks anthem, makes lewd gesture at baseball crowd

Roseanne Barr makes crude gesture after her mocking rendition of the National Anthem was booed by Padre fans in San Diego Wednesday night: Page 7

Associated Press

FEDS CLEAR DINKINS IN STOCK DEAL WITH SON Page Two

NEW YORK POST

METRO EDITION

MONDAY, OCTOBER 7, 1991 / Sunny, low 60s today; clear, low 50s tonight / Details, Page 2   R   40¢ in New York City **50¢** elsewhere

I do . . .
Conrad Hilton, Jr. Wed: 1950. Divorced: 1951.

I do . .
Michael Wilding. Wed: 1952. Divorced: 1957.

I do . .
Mike Todd. Wed: 1957. Died: 1958.

I do . .
Eddie Fisher. Wed: 1959. Divorced: 1964.

I do, I do .
Richard Burton. Wed: 1964. Divorced: 1974. Wed: 1975. Divorced: 1976.

I do . . .
John Warner. Wed: 1976. Divorced: 1982.

I DO!

Liz and Larry: *"It's like a dream."*   Liz Taylor ties the knot for the eight time: Page 5

O.J. SIMPSON EXTRA

NEW YORK POST

SPORTS EXTRA

SATURDAY, JUNE 18, SUNDAY, JUNE 19, 1994 / Humid and hot 90s today; Sunny 80s tomorrow with showers possible / Details, Page 20 ★   50¢

O.J.'s LAST RUN

Associated Press

Los Angeles police negotiated to get O.J. Simpson to give up after a desperate freeway chase last night.

BULLETIN

He gives up after desperate freeway chase back home

SIX PAGES INSIDE

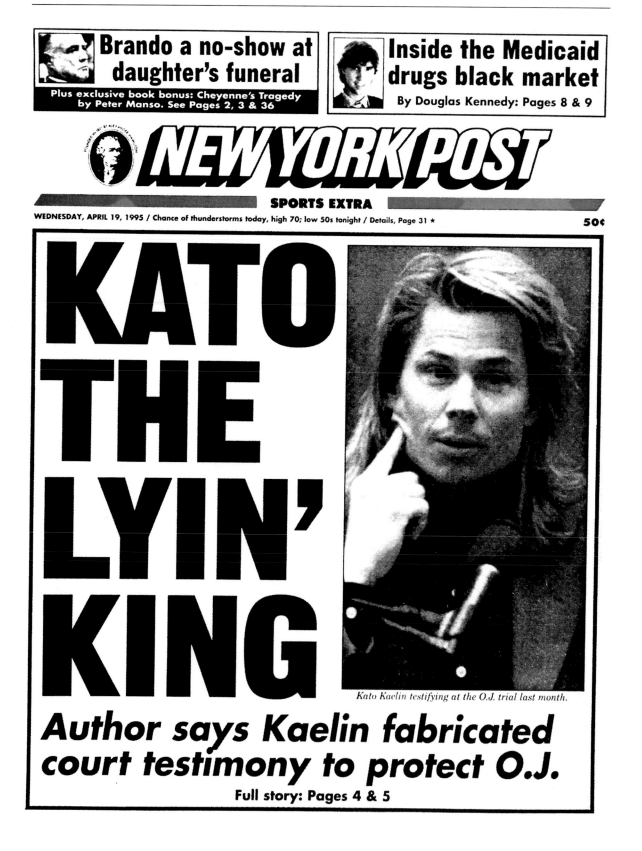

NEW YORK POST

SPORTS EXTRA

WEDNESDAY, APRIL 19, 1995 / Chance of thunderstorms today, high 70; low 50s tonight / Details, Page 31 ★   50¢

KATO THE LYIN' KING

Kato Kaelin testifying at the O.J. trial last month.

Author says Kaelin fabricated court testimony to protect O.J.

Full story: Pages 4 & 5

LATE CITY FINAL

THURSDAY, OCTOBER 12, 1995 / Sunny today, 83; clear and mild tonight, 58 / Details, Page 24 ★★

50¢

Photo composite by Dennis Wickman

Why O.J. wimped out

The inside story: See Pages 8, 9 & 18

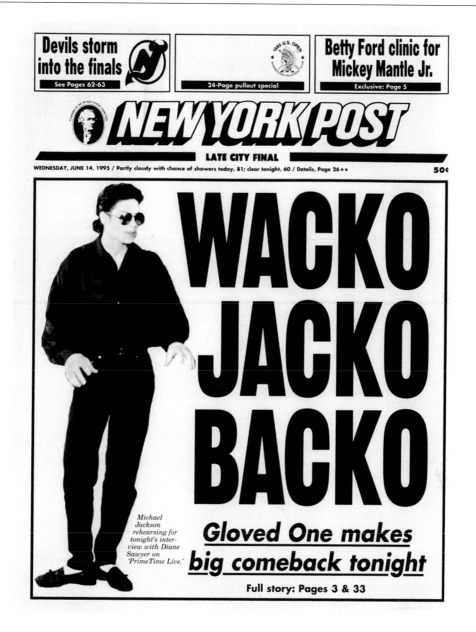

Devils storm into the finals
See Pages 62-63

1995 U.S. OPEN
24-Page pullout special

Betty Ford clinic for Mickey Mantle Jr.
Exclusive: Page 5

NEW YORK POST

LATE CITY FINAL

WEDNESDAY, JUNE 14, 1995 / Partly cloudy with chance of showers today, 81; clear tonight, 60 / Details, Page 26 ✶✶

50¢

WACKO JACKO BACKO

Michael Jackson rehearsing for tonight's interview with Diane Sawyer on 'PrimeTime Live.'

Gloved One makes big comeback tonight

Full story: Pages 3 & 33

Jacko

Here's a fair question: How many times must Michael Jackson be accused of consorting with young boys before it actually sticks?

And another fair question: Where did the sobriquet "Jacko" come from?

Let's face it: Jacko just isn't a name that falls gracefully on American ears. So what exactly is its origin?

The short answer is the British tabloids.

There are just some things that the English do extremely well (tailoring comes to mind). And, anyway, how do you identify this character in a very small space with very large type?

Suggestions are welcome.

SUNDAY

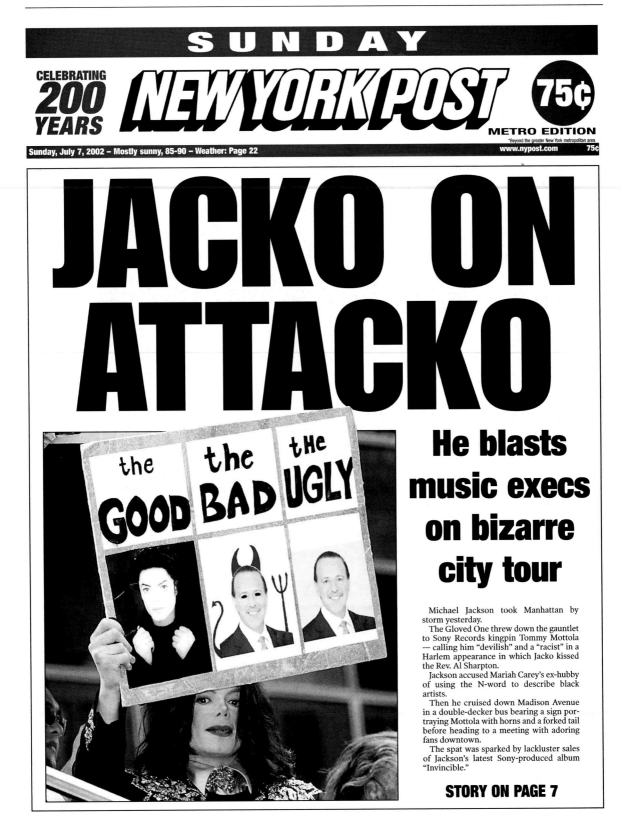

CELEBRATING
200
YEARS

NEW YORK POST

75¢

METRO EDITION

*Beyond the greater New York metropolitan area

Sunday, July 7, 2002 — Mostly sunny, 85-90 — Weather: Page 22

www.nypost.com   75¢

JACKO ON ATTACKO

the **GOOD** the **BAD** tHe **UGLY**

He blasts music execs on bizarre city tour

Michael Jackson took Manhattan by storm yesterday.

The Gloved One threw down the gauntlet to Sony Records kingpin Tommy Mottola — calling him "devilish" and a "racist" in a Harlem appearance in which Jacko kissed the Rev. Al Sharpton.

Jackson accused Mariah Carey's ex-hubby of using the N-word to describe black artists.

Then he cruised down Madison Avenue in a double-decker bus bearing a sign portraying Mottola with horns and a forked tail before heading to a meeting with adoring fans downtown.

The spat was sparked by lackluster sales of Jackson's latest Sony-produced album "Invincible."

STORY ON PAGE 7

FRIDAY, JUNE 3, 2005 / Cool; areas of drizzle and fog; a shower, 70 / Weather: Page 46   www.nypost.com   • • • • **50¢**

Jennifer Wilbanks in court yesterday.

Run, baby, run

Flee bride appears in court – in her running shoes

PAGE 3

SWEAT, FREAK

Jacko's fate goes to jury

PAGE 7

Getty Images

NEW YORK POST

25 CENTS

LATE CITY FINAL

TUESDAY, JUNE 14, 2005 / Partly sunny, hot and humid, 96 / Weather: Page 26 ★★   www.nypost.com   • • • • 25¢

Boy, oh, boy!

Jacko cleared of kid molest

HE BEAT IT

He beat it. Michael Jackson, here after the verdict, was acquitted yesterday of all charges that he molested a 13-year-old boy.

Jurors said they cleared Jacko, in part because they were turned off by the accuser's mother.

"I disliked it intensely when she snapped her fingers at us," said one. "Don't snap your fingers at me, lady."

JURORS — WE HATED MOM: Pages 2-7

Kevork Djansezian

U.S. push for Leb cease fire

Page 6

Cop killed in car-chase tragedy

Page 4

Council bigs: Nix term limits

Page 3

NEW YORK POST

SPECIAL 25¢ PRICE

LATE CITY FINAL

TUESDAY, APRIL 16, 1996 / Cloudy & windy today, 52; clearing skies tonight, 55 / Details, Page 22 ★★

LIZ SMITH EXCLUSIVE

Lionel Cherrault/SIPA Press

Just call her MAMA-DONNA

The stork's on its way to visit The Material Girl! Madonna is pregnant and a personal trainer she's known for 1 ½ years is the father. A Liz Smith exclusive: Pages 4 & 5

Raped Fordham co-ed wakes from coma : Page 6

China mourns death of Deng
PAGES 2 & 3

Pat urges probe of fund-raising
EXCLUSIVE: PAGE 4
Moynihan

Dems rip into Rudy
PAGES 6 & 7

New York Post

HOME DELIVERY
1-800-940-7678
CALL TODAY!

LATE CITY FINAL

THURSDAY, FEBRUARY 20, 1997 / Sunny, 45 / Weather: Page 61 ★★   http://www.nypostonline.com/   · · · 50¢

ABC slaps Walters over
$100G 'Sunset Blvd.' conflict

BABA BLACK SHEEP

FULL STORY: PAGE 5

ABC newswoman Barbara Walters was admonished by her own network yesterday for profiling composer Andrew Lloyd Webber but failing to tell viewers she invested $100,000 in his Broadway production of "Sunset Boulevard."

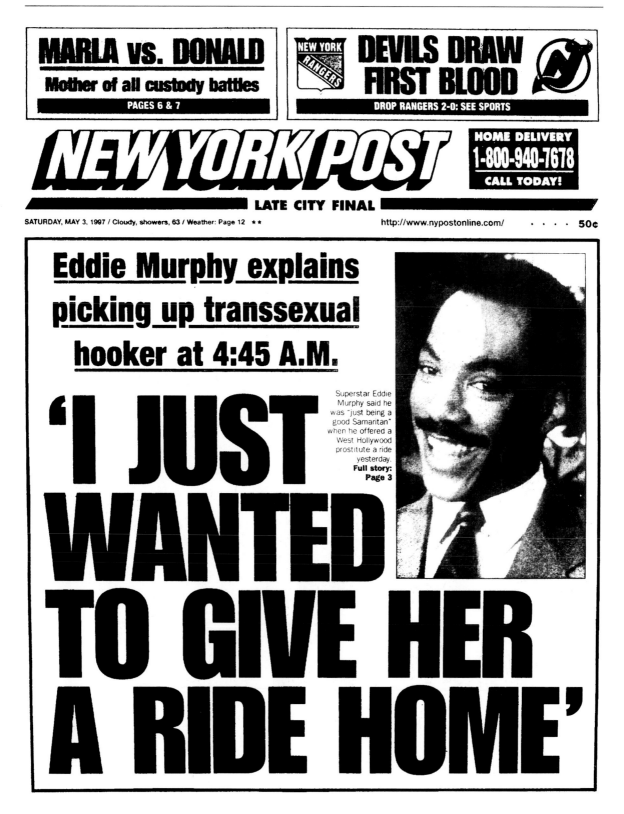

MARLA vs. DONALD
Mother of all custody battles
PAGES 6 & 7

NEW YORK RANGERS

DEVILS DRAW FIRST BLOOD
DROP RANGERS 2-0: SEE SPORTS

NEW YORK POST

HOME DELIVERY
1-800-940-7678
CALL TODAY!

LATE CITY FINAL

SATURDAY, MAY 3, 1997 / Cloudy, showers, 63 / Weather: Page 12 ★★   http://www.nypostonline.com/   · · · · 50¢

Eddie Murphy explains picking up transsexual hooker at 4:45 A.M.

Superstar Eddie Murphy said he was "just being a good Samaritan" when he offered a West Hollywood prostitute a ride yesterday.
Full story: Page 3

'I JUST WANTED TO GIVE HER A RIDE HOME'

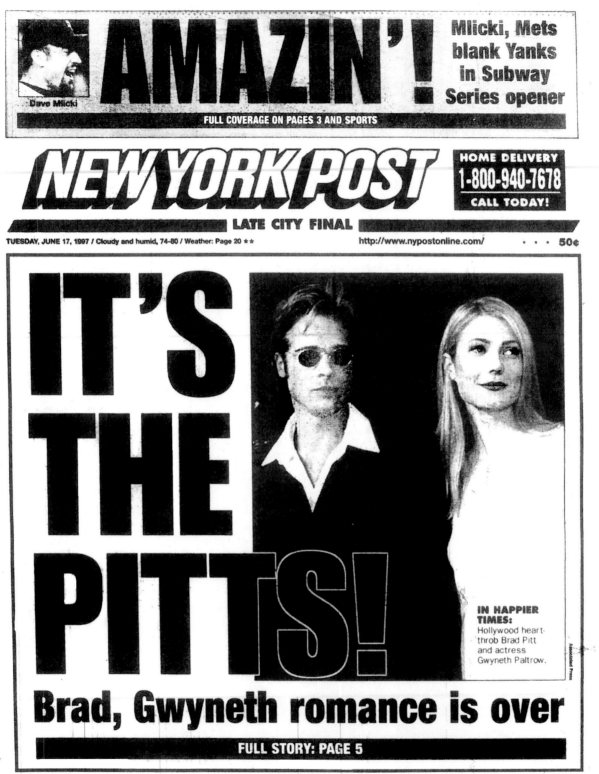

AMAZIN'!

Dave Mlicki

Mlicki, Mets blank Yanks in Subway Series opener

FULL COVERAGE ON PAGES 3 AND SPORTS

NEW YORK POST

HOME DELIVERY
1-800-940-7678
CALL TODAY!

LATE CITY FINAL

TUESDAY, JUNE 17, 1997 / Cloudy and humid, 74-80 / Weather: Page 20 ★★   http://www.nypostonline.com/   · · · 50¢

IT'S THE PITTS!

IN HAPPIER TIMES: Hollywood heart-throb Brad Pitt and actress Gwyneth Paltrow.

Brad, Gwyneth romance is over

FULL STORY: PAGE 5

NEW YORK POST

METRO EDITION

FRIDAY, FEBRUARY 6, 1998 / Morning clouds, afternoon sun, 45 / Weather: Page 73

http://www.nypostonline.com/

50¢

Muscled macho action-star decked at Scores

STORY: PAGE 6

JEAN-CLAUDE VAN SLAMMED!

NYers on Rudy's Civil War
Fuggedabowdit!
PAGES 6 & 7

Fed ax falls on Louima cops
Volpe
PAGES 2 & 3

NEW YORK POST

LATE CITY FINAL

FRIDAY, FEBRUARY 27, 1998 / Sunny, high 50s / Weather: Page 86   ★ ★   http://www.nypostonline.com/   50¢

A jubilant Oprah Winfrey reacts to verdict yesterday outside Texas courtroom.

OFF THE HOOF

THE GOOD NEWS: She beats beef rap

THE BAD NEWS: Her talk show reign is threatened by Jerry Springer

FULL STORY: PAGE 5

THE WOMAN ON KEVORKIAN'S ARM

My date with Doctor Death

PAGE 7

Dr. Jack Kevorkian and Rebecca Eaton at N.Y. gala.

NEW YORK POST

HOME DELIVERY
1-800-940-7678
CALL TODAY!

LATE CITY FINAL

THURSDAY, MARCH 5, 1998 / Cloudy, 44-48 / Weather: Page 70 ★★   http://www.nypostonline.com/   · · · · **50¢**

FOSTER MOM

Oscar winner Jodie Foster at a function in Manhattan the other night.

Jodie pregnant – but she's mum on the dad

LIZ SMITH EXCLUSIVE: PAGE 3

Rikers teacher suspended for hitting inmate PAGE 4

NEW YORK POST

LATE CITY FINAL

THURSDAY, APRIL 9, 1998 / Windy with heavy rain, 52 / Weather: Page 112 ★★   http://www.nypostonline.com/   • 50¢

L.A. cop busts George Michael for 'lewd act'

DOWN AND OUTED IN BEVERLY HILLS

Pop legend George Michael

SPECIAL REPORT

COMPLETE COVERAGE BEGINS ON PAGES 4 & 5

HILL SNUBS DUBYA
Rejects invite to White House
PAGE 3

My Lai pilot: Kerrey should go to jail
PAGE 7

CELEBRATING **200** YEARS

NEW YORK POST

25 CENTS

LATE CITY FINAL

FRIDAY, APRIL 27, 2001 / Partly cloudy, chance of late-day shower, 72 / Weather: Page 65 ★★   www.nypost.com   V • • • • **25¢**

HEADLINE NUDES

Andrea Thompson, former "NYPD Blue" star who just landed a job at CNN Headline News, says she's not ashamed of taking it all off.

CNN defends new anchor in steamy photos flap

PAGE 5

Brawlin' Baldwins duke it out with fan at Knicks game PAGE 9

CELEBRATING 200 YEARS

NEW YORK POST

LATE CITY FINAL

25 CENTS

TUESDAY, JANUARY 14, 2003 / Partly cloudy, 30 / Weather: Page 28 ★★   www.nypost.com   • • • • 25¢

WHO, ME?

Dan Charlty

Rock legend in child porn arrest

By MARSHA KRANES

Legendary rock star Pete Townshend of The Who (above, right after being taken into custody), was hauled off by Scotland Yard detectives last night to face child-pornography charges.

Townshend, 57, appearing haggard and unshaven, was led out a side door of his sprawling digs in southwest London and driven to a nearby police station.

He was detained on suspicion of making and possessing indecent images of children, and of inciting others to distribute kiddie

See **TOWNSHEND** Page 2

EXCLUSIVE: FEDS REVEAL NYC BOMB PLOT — See page 4

NEW YORK POST

25 CENTS

LATE CITY FINAL

TUESDAY, FEBRUARY 3, 2004 / Snow and sleet changing to rain, 42 / Weather: Page 52 ★★   www.nypost.com   • • • • **25¢**

Justin Timberlake grabs Janet Jackson's leather jacket moments before pulling it away to expose her breast at the Super Bowl.

EPA/Rhona Wise

Tit for tat

TV chiefs plan Grammy ban for stars

FULL STORY: PAGES 6-7

NEW YORK POST

25 CENTS

LATE CITY FINAL

TUESDAY, MARCH 9, 2004 / Variable clouds and cold, 45 / Weather: Page 28 ★★   www.nypost.com   • • • •   25¢

Sex secrets of a single mom

ANGELINA JOLIE EXCLUSIVE: PAGE 41

HUMBLE PIE

Shame of Martha's new ordeal

Martha Stewart suffered the indignities of the common criminal yesterday — right down to the mandatory urine test — when she visited her probation officer at Manhattan federal court.

The prison-bound goddess of good-living appeared on a day as bleak as her future and was forced to tell the feds such intimate personal details as how much she spends on clothing and groceries.

FULL STORY: PAGES 4-5

N.Y. Post: G.N. Miller

River corpse identified as Spalding Gray PAGE 7

NEW YORK POST

HOME DELIVERY
1-800-552-7678
CALL TODAY!

LATE CITY FINAL

SATURDAY, JULY 17, 2004 / Warmer with some sun; a p.m. t-shower, 86 / Weather: Page 62 ★★   www.nypost.com   · · · · **50¢**

NICE SUIT

Martha gets five months in the pen; reveals her shame

A shamed Martha Stewart choked back tears and pleaded for leniency at her sentencing yesterday, and she got it — five months in prison, five months of house arrest and the freedom to stay out of jail pending appeal.

"Today is a shameful day," the usually self-assured celebrity homemaker told the court.

FULL STORY: PAGES 4, 5, 6, 7, 8, 9

GO TO JAIL

Post composite by Peter LaVigna

Hastro Monopoly

NEW YORK POST

25 CENTS

LATE CITY FINAL

THURSDAY, SEPTEMBER 30, 2004 / Chance of a shower this afternoon, 70 / Weather: Page 34 ★ ★ X   www.nypost.com   • • • •   25¢

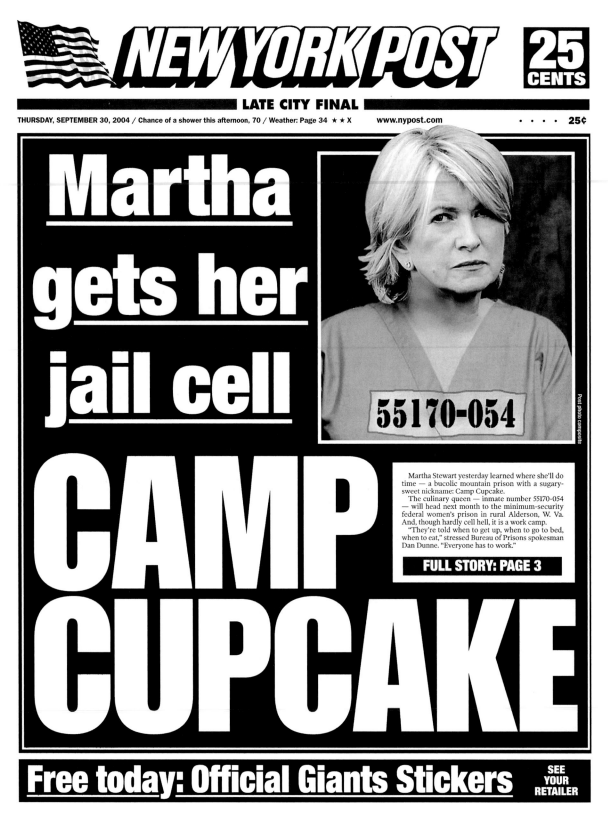

Martha gets her jail cell

55170-054

Post photo composite

CAMP CUPCAKE

Martha Stewart yesterday learned where she'll do time — a bucolic mountain prison with a sugary-sweet nickname: Camp Cupcake.

The culinary queen — inmate number 55170-054 — will head next month to the minimum-security federal women's prison in rural Alderson, W. Va. And, though hardly cell hell, it is a work camp.

"They're told when to get up, when to go to bed, when to eat," stressed Bureau of Prisons spokesman Dan Dunne. "Everyone has to work."

FULL STORY: PAGE 3

Free today: Official Giants Stickers

SEE YOUR RETAILER

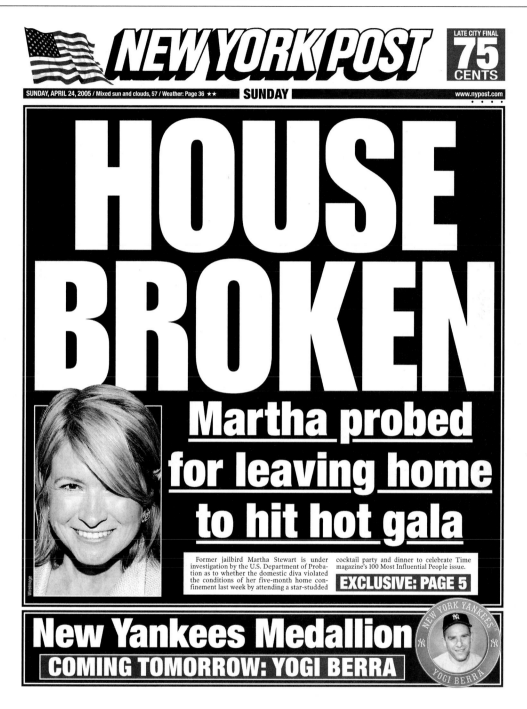

NEW YORK POST

LATE CITY FINAL
75 CENTS

SUNDAY, APRIL 24, 2005 / Mixed sun and clouds, 57 / Weather: Page 36 ★★   **SUNDAY**   www.nypost.com

HOUSE BROKEN

Martha probed for leaving home to hit hot gala

Former jailbird Martha Stewart is under investigation by the U.S. Department of Probation as to whether the domestic diva violated the conditions of her five-month home confinement last week by attending a star-studded cocktail party and dinner to celebrate Time magazine's 100 Most Influential People issue.

EXCLUSIVE: PAGE 5

Wireimage

New Yankees Medallion
COMING TOMORROW: YOGI BERRA

NEW YORK YANKEES
YOGI BERRA

House Broken

There were a lot of people who felt sorry for Martha Stewart when she was caught dumping stock. *The Post* obviously wasn't among them.

If it raises any of life's questions, one would be, "How much money do you need?" Or, to flip Gordon Gekko's mantra, "Greed is not good."

So this was our response in the Sunday *Post* when she was ordered under house arrest. After all, Stewart is the Domestic Diva.

NEW YORK POST

25 CENTS

LATE CITY FINAL

FRIDAY, SEPTEMBER 17, 2004 / A shower or thunderstorm; humid, 80 / Weather: Page 29 ★★   www.nypost.com   · · · ·   25¢

$3.50 plus tax

NEW YORK GIANTS
2004 OFFICIAL STICKER COLLECTION

NEW YORK POST

Giants, Jets, sticker albums

$3.50 plus tax

NEW YORK JETS
2004 OFFICIAL STICKER COLLECTION

NEW YORK POST

Get yours today: Coupons, Pages 18-19

FREE STICKERS START MONDAY

BEDLAM IN THE BRONX

SEE SPORTS

A DAN SHAME

White House slaps Rather

STORY: PAGE 6

NEW YORK POST

25 CENTS

LATE CITY FINAL

THURSDAY, JULY 7, 2005 / Limited sun; a stray p.m. thunderstorm, 80 / Weather: Page 67 ★★   www.nypost.com   • • • • 25¢

LIL' JAIL TIME

Gets off easy as judge cites Martha

Lil' Kim is going to the Big House.

A federal judge yesterday slapped the risqué rapper with a year and a day in prison for perjury — but spared her a possible 3 1/2 years after comparing her to another high-profile celebrity liar, Martha Stewart.

The judge asked out loud how the public would react to a black entertainer getting a stiffer sentence than the Domestic Diva got for lying.

Kim, dressed demurely — pictured here after the sentencing — admitted to the court for the first time that she had lied under oath while covering up for pals in a gunfight.

FULL STORY: PAGE 5

Reuters

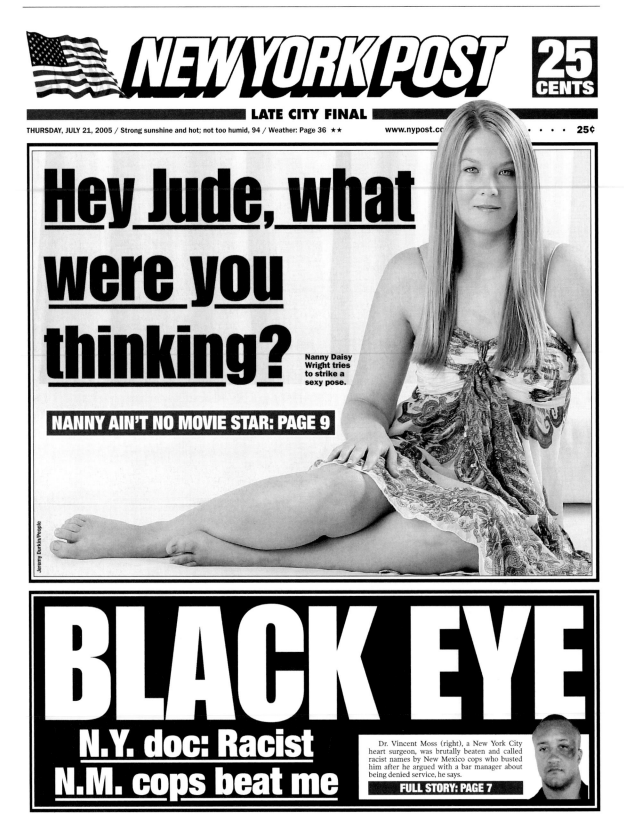

Hey Jude, what were you thinking?

Nanny Daisy Wright tries to strike a sexy pose.

NANNY AIN'T NO MOVIE STAR: PAGE 9

Jeremy Durkin/People

BLACK EYE

N.Y. doc: Racist N.M. cops beat me

Dr. Vincent Moss (right), a New York City heart surgeon, was brutally beaten and called racist names by New Mexico cops who busted him after he argued with a bar manager about being denied service, he says.

FULL STORY: PAGE 7

NEW YORK POST

ONLY 50¢

METRO EDITION

SATURDAY, OCTOBER 8, 2005 / Rain, some heavy; breezy and humid, 74 / Weather: Page 20   www.nypost.com   • • • • 50¢

Red Sox socked
SEE SPORTS

Subway jitters
PAGES 4-5

BAD BOY

Star in N.Y. coke bust

British singer Boy George was arrested yesterday after he called police to his SoHo apartment on a false burglary call and they found a mound of cocaine. Cops said they found the door open and were greeted by the 44-year-old singer, who appeared high and asked them, "What's up?"

STORY: PAGE 3

Wacky Boy George (pictured in '03) is in a sweat over his arrest.

POST POKER NEW GAME CARD MONDAY

NEW YORK POST

ONLY 50¢

METRO EDITION

SATURDAY, NOVEMBER 19, 2005 / Chilly with plenty of sunshine, 50 / Weather: Page 67   www.nypost.com   · · · ·   **50¢**

Jury: Blake killed wife

FULL STORY: PAGE 9

POST POKER

TODAY'S NUMBERS: PAGE 67

NEW GAME CARD MONDAY

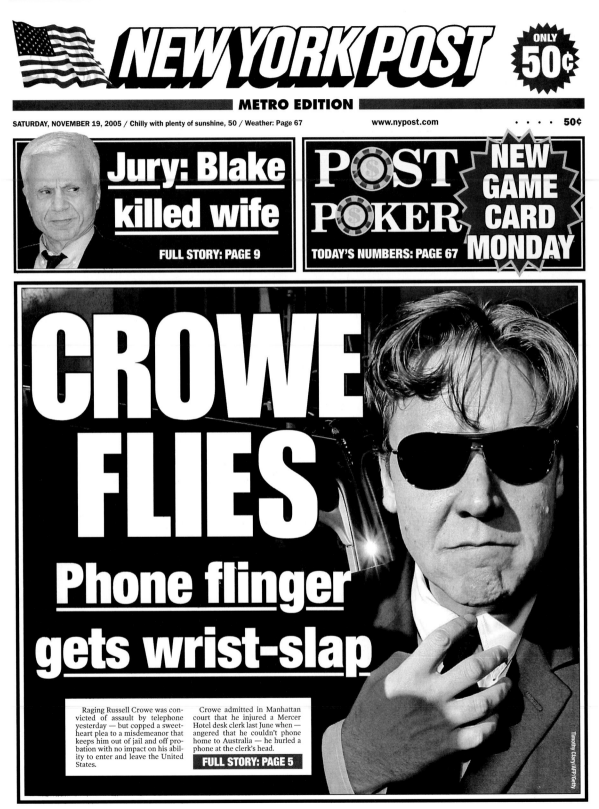

CROWE FLIES

Phone flinger gets wrist-slap

Raging Russell Crowe was convicted of assault by telephone yesterday — but copped a sweetheart plea to a misdemeanor that keeps him out of jail and off probation with no impact on his ability to enter and leave the United States.

Crowe admitted in Manhattan court that he injured a Mercer Hotel desk clerk last June when — angered that he couldn't phone home to Australia — he hurled a phone at the clerk's head.

FULL STORY: PAGE 5

Timothy Clary/AFP/Getty

NEW YORK POST

NOT FOR RESALE

PROMOTIONAL COPY

WEDNESDAY, NOVEMBER 29, 2006 / Mild; overcast, then some sun, 64 / Weather: Page 36 X   www.nypost.com   · · · ·

Bimbo summit

It's a meeting of the minds as best pals Lindsay Lohan, Britney Spears and Paris Hilton leave an L.A. late-night spot.   **SEE PULSE: PAGE 39**

JUDGE & FURY

Mike has cop 'trial' all set up

By DAVID SEIFMAN

A day after claiming police used "excessive force" in the strip-club car shooting that left an unarmed man dead on his wedding day, Mayor Bloomberg yesterday said he was speaking only as "a civilian" — but then stated he wants the cops tried in Queens. Responding to crit-
See **MAYOR** *Page 4*

NEW YORK POST 75¢

50 SHOTS

Police kill groom on wedding day

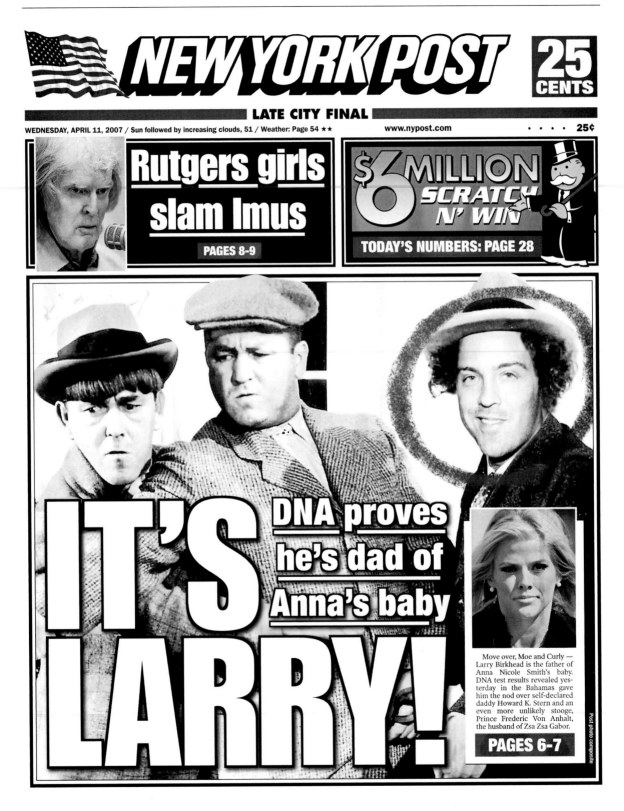

NEW YORK POST

25 CENTS

LATE CITY FINAL

WEDNESDAY, APRIL 11, 2007 / Sun followed by increasing clouds, 51 / Weather: Page 54 ★★   www.nypost.com   • • • •   25¢

Rutgers girls slam Imus
PAGES 8-9

$6 MILLION SCRATCH N' WIN
TODAY'S NUMBERS: PAGE 28

IT'S LARRY!

DNA proves he's dad of Anna's baby

Move over, Moe and Curly — Larry Birkhead is the father of Anna Nicole Smith's baby. DNA test results revealed yesterday in the Bahamas gave him the nod over self-declared daddy Howard K. Stern and an even more unlikely stooge, Prince Frederic Von Anhalt, the husband of Zsa Zsa Gabor.

PAGES 6-7

Post photo composite

FRIDAY, JUNE 8, 2007 / Mostly sunny, hot and humid, 92 / Weather: Page 32 ★★   www.nypost.com   · · · · 25¢

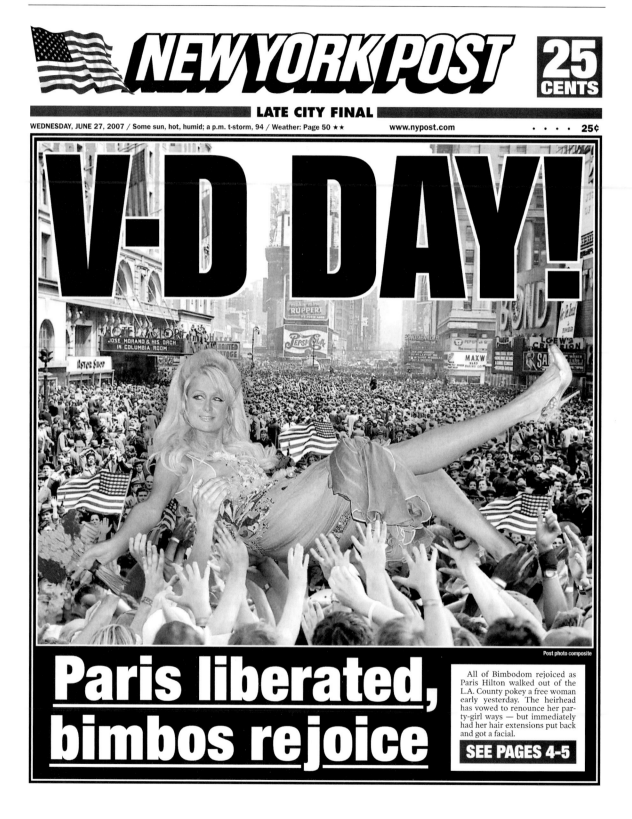

NEW YORK POST

LATE CITY FINAL

WEDNESDAY, JUNE 27, 2007 / Some sun, hot, humid; a p.m. t-storm, 94 / Weather: Page 50 ★★   www.nypost.com   • • • •   25¢

25 CENTS

V-D DAY!

Post photo composite

Paris liberated, bimbos rejoice

All of Bimbodom rejoiced as Paris Hilton walked out of the L.A. County pokey a free woman early yesterday. The heirhead has vowed to renounce her party-girl ways — but immediately had her hair extensions put back and got a facial.

SEE PAGES 4-5

25 CENTS

LATE CITY FINAL

WEDNESDAY, NOVEMBER 28, 2007 / Mostly sunny, 50 / Weather: Page 20 ★★   www.nypost.com   · · · · 25¢

ASTOR FORTUNE SCANDAL

BAD HEIR DAY

Inside DA's case against Brooke's son

Brooke Astor's weeping son was arraigned yesterday on charges of looting her $198 million estate.

Anthony Marshall, here on his way to court yesterday, used the ill-gotten gains to buy a 55-foot yacht and pay its captain, Manhattan prosecutors charge.

PAGES 6 & 7

Steven Hirsch

SPORTS

One-time challenger Mitch "Blood" Green (left) shows his facial stitches after coming off the loser in a dawn encounter with Tyson (above), who ruefully nurses broken hand.

NEW YORK POST

Monday Sports Special

22 Pages

JUNE 30, 1997

Losing the fight brought out the punk in Tyson

BITE OF THE CENTURY

Mike Tyson lets fangs show after being disqualified from Saturday night's title fight for biting Evander Holyfield twice, once on each ear. For complete coverage of boxing's latest disgrace, see Pages 2-5 and 76-73.

WALLACE MATTHEWS / PAGE 5

TINO HELPS BOMBERS TRIP TRIBE

BROOKS, MARTIN
PAGES 83-80

JOEL SHERMAN

BRAVES BACK FOR SEQUEL TO SERIES

PAGE 80

AMAZIN'S POUND BUCS WITH 5 HRs

WALDSTEIN / PAGE 78

TONIGHT ON **MSG** — IT'S A WORLD SERIES REMATCH — YANKEES VS. BRAVES - 7:30PM

1427

Tyson Bites Holyfield

In the world of the sports desk, unstable is good; full-on nuts is even better. So good ol' Mike Tyson has never let us down.

"Tyson's bite fight" was the gift that kept on giving, recalls one sports desk guy. "It was a comedy of the absurd. But maybe not so funny to Holyfield."

At the bout's outset, the attending *Post* re-porters were expecting a fight as routine as any other belt match. The first two rounds confirmed their expectations.

But in the third round, the two reporters breathlessly called in from Vegas, one shouting, "He bit off a piece of Holyfield's ear! Tyson totally snapped!"

So did Evander's ear.

Tyson's chomp was headline fodder for days.

World reacts to Tyson's boxing ban:

'EAR 'EAR!

JACK NEWFIELD, WALLACE MATTHEWS: PAGES 2 & 3

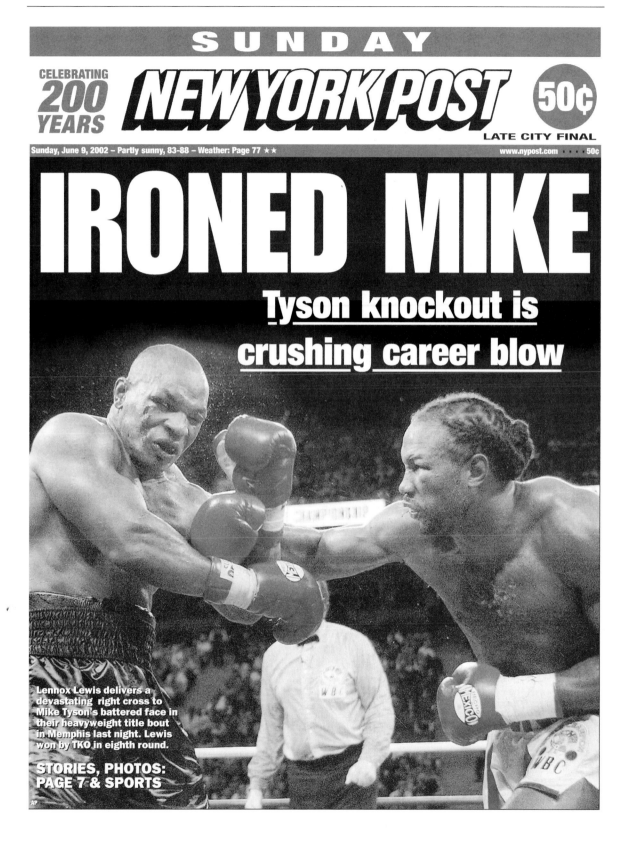

NEW YORK POST

CELEBRATING 200 YEARS

50¢

LATE CITY FINAL

Sunday, June 9, 2002 – Partly sunny, 83-88 – Weather: Page 77 ★ ★

www.nypost.com · · · · 50¢

IRONED MIKE

Tyson knockout is crushing career blow

Lennox Lewis delivers a devastating right cross to Mike Tyson's battered face in their heavyweight title bout in Memphis last night. Lewis won by TKO in eighth round.

**STORIES, PHOTOS:
PAGE 7 & SPORTS**

AP

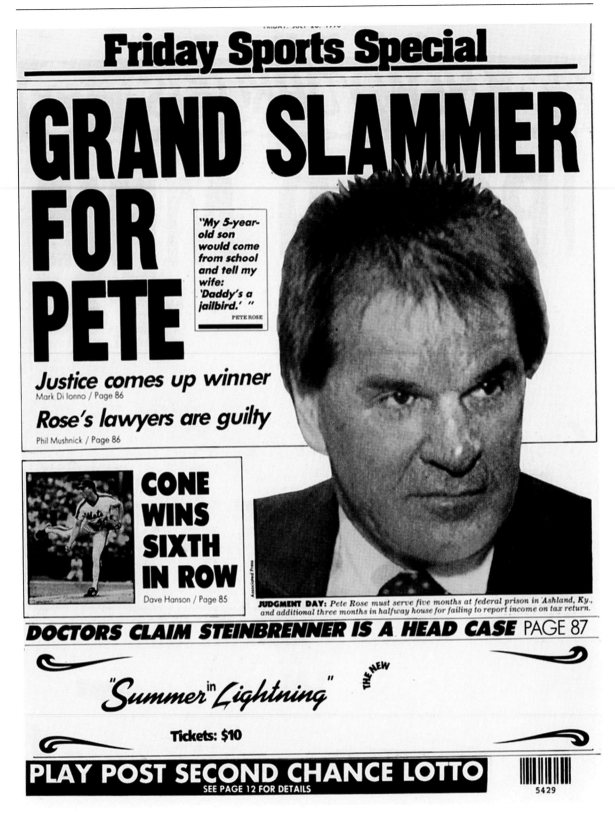

Friday Sports Special

GRAND SLAMMER FOR PETE

"My 5-year-old son would come from school and tell my wife: 'Daddy's a jailbird.'"

PETE ROSE

Justice comes up winner
Mark Di Ionno / Page 86

Rose's lawyers are guilty
Phil Mushnick / Page 86

CONE WINS SIXTH IN ROW
Dave Hanson / Page 85

JUDGMENT DAY: Pete Rose must serve five months at federal prison in Ashland, Ky., and additional three months in halfway house for failing to report income on tax return.

DOCTORS CLAIM STEINBRENNER IS A HEAD CASE PAGE 87

"Summer in Lightning" THE NEW

Tickets: $10

PLAY POST SECOND CHANCE LOTTO
SEE PAGE 12 FOR DETAILS

5429

MONDAY, JULY 29, 1991

NEW YORK POST
Sports

Dennis Martinez

MONTREAL'S MARTINEZ THROWS PERFECT GAME AGAINST DODGERS

Details / Page 51

BUSTED!

Kamieniecki gets wracked after stripper pays visit to mound

Angels soar past Yanks: Charlie McCarthy / Page 52

STEAL MAGNOLIA: *Padres' Craig Shipley looks on as Vince Coleman bags his 14th stolen base of season during eighth inning of Mets' 2-0 loss yesterday in San Diego. John Harper has details on Page 53.*

DOUBLE TROUBLE: *Yanks' Scott Kamieniecki got unexpected visitor to mound yesterday during 8-4 loss to Angels at the Stadium — "Toppsy Curvey," aptly named exotic dancer who's got her sights set on becoming next Morganna, baseball's infamous "Kissing Bandit."*

1130

FRIDAY AUGUST 16, 1991

Friday Sports Special

NEW YORK POST

METS FALL
John Harper / P. 91

Don, benched for long hair, looks to cut Yank ties

PLAY BALD!

STEVE SERBY

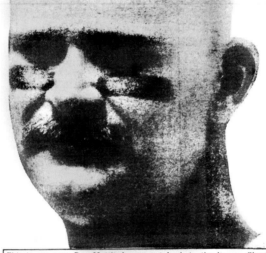

MARK KRIEGEL

Blame Michael as fur flies in the Bronx Zoo

ST. LOUIS — Doc Gooden sat at his locker in the Mets' clubhouse at Busch Stadium last night and couldn't believe his ears.

Don Mattingly had been benched? For hair too long? DON MATTINGLY?

"What?" Gooden asked, eyes bugging out of his head. "Are you serious? Aw, c'mon."

Then Doc Gooden said, "I'd rather not get into that. That's over in The Bronx. I never heard nothing like that."

Informed that Mattingly had asked to be traded earlier this year, Gooden said with a smile: "I think we can make a move for him."

The more Doc Gooden thought about it, the more incredulous he became. "I can see if a rookie got called up and had a long pony-

See **SERBY** Page 90

It's hair today, gone tomorrow for Mattingly

HOW stupid was this? How miserably stupid?

Here we have New York's best baseball player since Mickey Mantle, and he is benched and fined because his hair is too long.

The New York Mets have become a terrible baseball team, in large part because they have no one like Don Mattingly. But the Yankees, in their infinite wisdom, decide they can do without him. "Rules are rules," they say. The Yankee administrators, who should be concerned with nothing but rebuilding a baseball team, show themselves for schoolmarms. Rules are rules, kids, no matter how stupid. Donnie needs a haircut.

Idiots. Like this will bring a pennant to The Bronx. Like they don't have enough to worry

See **KRIEGEL** Page 90

This is one way Don Mattingly can get back in the lineup Charlie McCarthy has all the details on Yankee star's benching on Page 90

PLAY POST SECOND CHANCE LOTTO
SEE PAGE 41 FOR DETAILS

FOUNDED IN 1801 BY ALEXANDER HAMILTON

NEW YORK POST

LATE CITY FINAL

TUESDAY, MARCH 17, 1992 ★★ / Mostly cloudy, mid 40s today; clear, low 30s tonight / Details, Page 2

40¢ in New York City 50¢ elsewhere

Mets, beer, bikinis and . . .

SWING TRAINING

PORT ST. LUCIE, Fla. — A woman in a Mets cap and a suntan shakes everything she's got — determined to keep three Hula Hoops circling her bare midriff.

The band strikes up something raunchy. "When's the last time you made love?" the singer yells.

Suddenly, the doors swing wide open and in walks royalty: David Cone — Bret Saberhagen — Daryl Boston — real live Mets! Babes! Beer! Ballplayers!

Just another night — another

ANDREA PEYSER

rip-roaring rockin' good time — at Cruzan's Liquor Stand.

Like a cold blast from the North, baseball descends each spring on this desolate stretch of

eroding beach and swamp 60 miles north of tony Palm Beach — transforming it into a frenzied tropical playground.

Girls in tight shorts march in spike heels through the land of the blue-haired retirees. Young men in neon orange drive fast cars from beer barn to beach bars.

It's a culture of abbreviated clothes and beautiful bodies where the deepest conversation you'll find is about the surf.

It's a place where the men are ranked according to whether they play in the majors or the minors and the women are ranked according to the men they're with.

In this scene of fleshy competition a 31-year-old New York woman claims she was raped by three Mets. But at Cruzan's, where women are replaceable and ballplayers can do no wrong.

See SCENE on Page 5

EVERYONE GETS THEIR IRISH UP!

Extra cops for St. Patrick's Day parade as judge rules gay group can't march: Details on Page 4

FOUNDED IN 1801 BY ALEXANDER HAMILTON

NEW YORK POST

LATE CITY FINAL

FRIDAY, AUGUST 28, 1992 / Mostly cloudy, mid 80s today; showers likely, low 70s tonight / Details, Page 2 ★★   40¢ in New York City 50¢ elsewhere

CONE HEAD DEAL

DAVID CONE
Toronto-bound.

Mets fans in a rage over ace's trade for 2 unknowns

DETAILS: Pages 5, 86 & 87

Mets GM Al Harazin, who made the deal, claims it's simple economics.

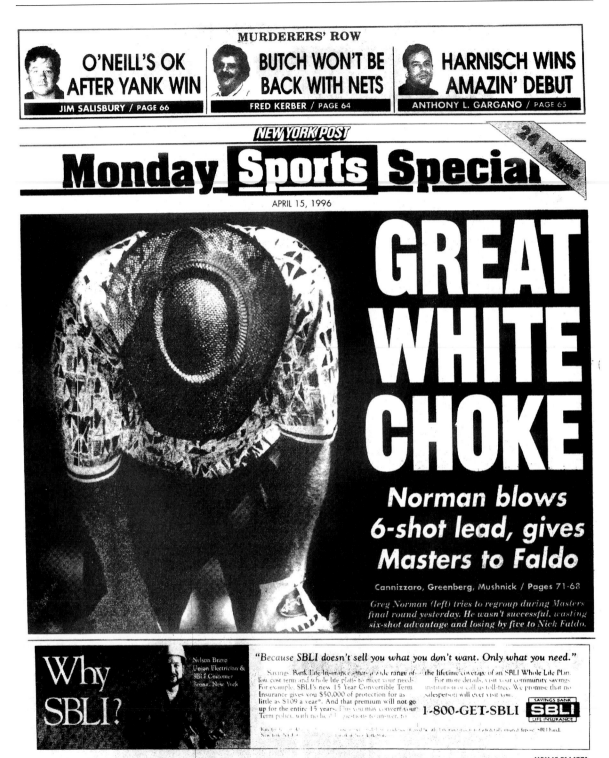

NEW YORK POST

Monday Sports Special

24 Pages

APRIL 15, 1996

GREAT WHITE CHOKE

Norman blows 6-shot lead, gives Masters to Faldo

Cannizzaro, Greenberg, Mushnick / Pages 71-68

Greg Norman (left) tries to regroup during Masters final round yesterday. He wasn't successful, wasting six-shot advantage and losing by five to Nick Faldo.

1416

Friday Sports Special

NEW YORK POST

FEBRUARY 14, 1997

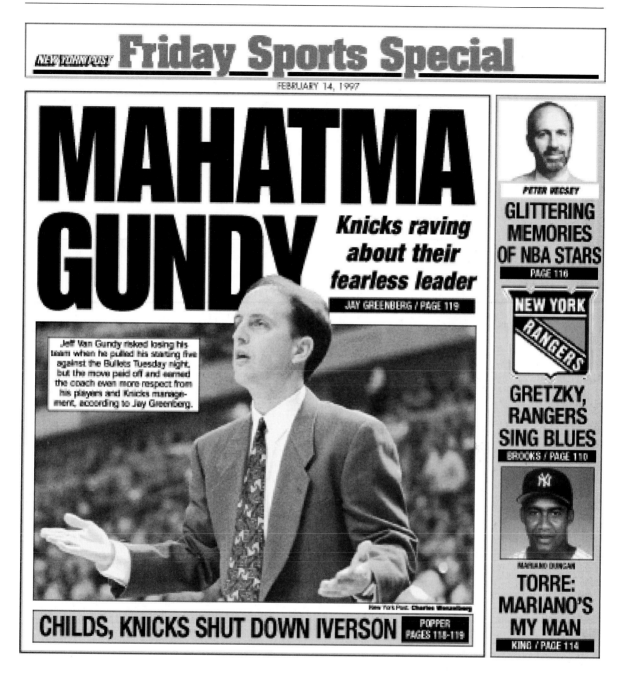

MAHATMA GUNDY

Knicks raving about their fearless leader

JAY GREENBERG / PAGE 119

Jeff Van Gundy risked losing his team when he pulled his starting five against the Bullets Tuesday night, but the move paid off and earned the coach even more respect from his players and Knicks management, according to Jay Greenberg.

New York Post: Charles Wenzelberg

CHILDS, KNICKS SHUT DOWN IVERSON
POPPER
PAGES 118-119

PETER VECSEY

GLITTERING MEMORIES OF NBA STARS
PAGE 116

NEW YORK RANGERS

GRETZKY, RANGERS SING BLUES
BROOKS / PAGE 110

MARIANO DUNCAN

TORRE: MARIANO'S MY MAN
KING / PAGE 114

REUNITED

ANGUISHED MOM GETS HER BABY BACK: PAGES 4 & 5

Annette Sorensen with daughter Liv

NEW YORK POST

HOME DELIVERY
1-800-940-7678
CALL TODAY!

LATE CITY FINAL

THURSDAY, MAY 15, 1997 / Morning showers, then partly cloudy, 70 / Weather: Page 58 ★★   http://www.nypostonline.com/   • • • •   **50¢**

FLIPPED OUT!

Knicks can't take Heat in Game 5 basketbrawl

PLAYOFF COVERAGE: SEE SPORTS

John Starks gives Miami crowd a piece of his mind last night as the Knicks fell 96-81 to the Heat. Knick players, including Starks, Charlie Ward, Larry Johnson and Allan Houston, face suspensions after leaving the bench to join an on-court brawl late in the fourth quarter.

BRING ON PHILLY!

Win hockey playoff tickets

FIND OUT HOW
ON PAGE 81

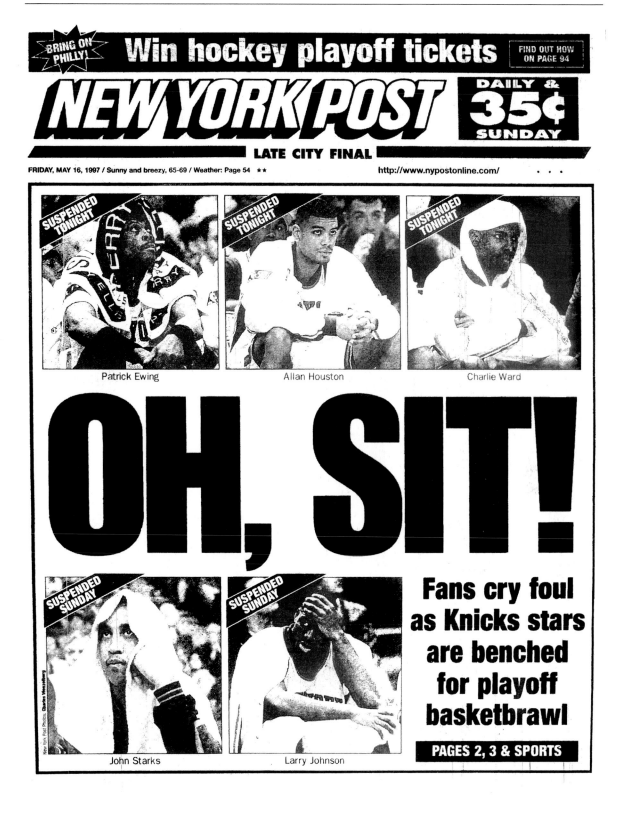

NEW YORK POST

DAILY & **35¢** SUNDAY

LATE CITY FINAL

FRIDAY, MAY 16, 1997 / Sunny and breezy, 65-69 / Weather: Page 54 ★★   http://www.nypostonline.com/   • • •

SUSPENDED TONIGHT

Patrick Ewing

SUSPENDED TONIGHT

Allan Houston

SUSPENDED TONIGHT

Charlie Ward

OH, SIT!

SUSPENDED SUNDAY

John Starks

SUSPENDED SUNDAY

Larry Johnson

Fans cry foul as Knicks stars are benched for playoff basketbrawl

PAGES 2, 3 & SPORTS

BEAST OF THE FAR EAST

COVERAGE BEGINS ON PAGE 118

Irabu earns 'Stripes with win, nine Ks in debut

Hideki Irabu waves to adoring crowd after leaving game in seventh inning of 10-3 win over Tigers at Stadium last night. Japanese phenom fanned nine in 6²/₃ innings in his major league debut.

New York Post **Charles Wenzelberg**

Mets **AMAZIN' LATE RALLY BATTERS BRAVES**

WALDSTEIN, KEEGAN / PAGES 114,115

One of the Great New York Traditions... Yankees Old Timers Day

TOMORROW ON...
OLD TIMERS DAY FESTIVITIES
BEGIN AT 2:00PM
YANKEES VS. TIGERS • 4:00PM
TONIGHT YANKEES VS. TIGERS • 7:30PM

MSG

Let The Games Begin... See Today's "Casino Gaming" Special Section On Page 61

5428

Playoff dream ends for Mets SEE SPORTS

Rolling Stones rock U.S. World tour opens in Chicago
Mick Jagger
SEE DAN AQUILANTE'S REVIEW: PAGES 43 & 45

NEW YORK POST
DAILY & 35¢ SUNDAY
LATE CITY FINAL
WEDNESDAY, SEPTEMBER 24, 1997 / Sunny, 60-65 / Weather: Page 26 ✱✱
http://www.nypostonline.com/

MARV BITES BACK

Sportscaster's accuser caught in 'bribe' try

COMPLETE COVERAGE BEGINS ON PAGE 2

Play-by-play man Marv Albert arrives at court in Virginia yesterday for his sexual assault trial.

Marv Albert

With his rapid-fire patter, distinctive voice, and trademark "Yes!", Marv Albert was one of the most famous play-by-play basketball broadcasters around. In addition to being the voice of the New York Knicks, his longtime stint as WNBC-TV's lead sportscaster led to national appearances on *Today* and the *Late Show with David Letterman*.

But in 1997, Albert's mouth landed him in a spot of trouble . . . in the bedroom. New Yorkers were shocked to learn that he was being charged with biting and forcibly sodomizing a woman with whom he'd enjoyed a 10-year sexual relationship. The case had all the trappings of a kinky novel: threesomes, phone sex, transvestites and cross-dressing (Albert reportedly wore women's panties while they coupled).

The headlines practically wrote themselves:

When Albert's lawyers went on the offensive in response to the charges, the front page blared "Marv Bites Back"; later, after accuser Vanessa Perhach's apparance in court, the Post ran the headline "The Kink & I."

The highlight (or lowlight) of the whole affair came when another woman, a hotel employee, claimed that Albert forced himself on her and she managed to escape by pulling off his toupee. The Post's headline: "The Night Marv Flipped His Wig." (Albert denied the story, saying he actually wore a hair weave that could not be removed.)

Eventually, DNA testing tripped Albert up— the bite marks on Perhach's back were indeed his. He pled guilty to misdemeanor charges and received a 12-month suspended sentence. Yes!

For *The Post*, it was a story with teeth to it.

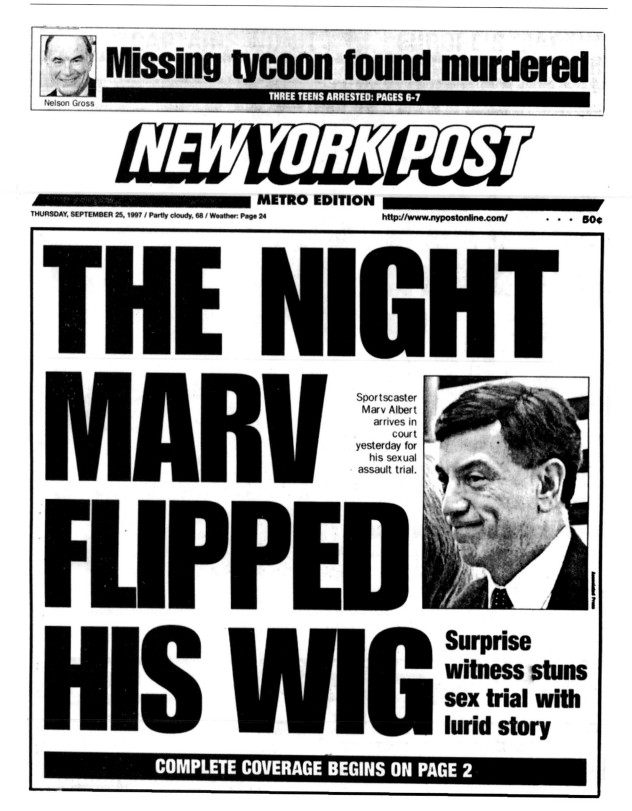

Missing tycoon found murdered

THREE TEENS ARRESTED: PAGES 6-7

Nelson Gross

NEW YORK POST

METRO EDITION

THURSDAY, SEPTEMBER 25, 1997 / Partly cloudy, 68 / Weather: Page 24

http://www.nypostonline.com/   · · · 50¢

THE NIGHT MARV FLIPPED HIS WIG

Sportscaster Marv Albert arrives in court yesterday for his sexual assault trial.

Surprise witness stuns sex trial with lurid story

COMPLETE COVERAGE BEGINS ON PAGE 2

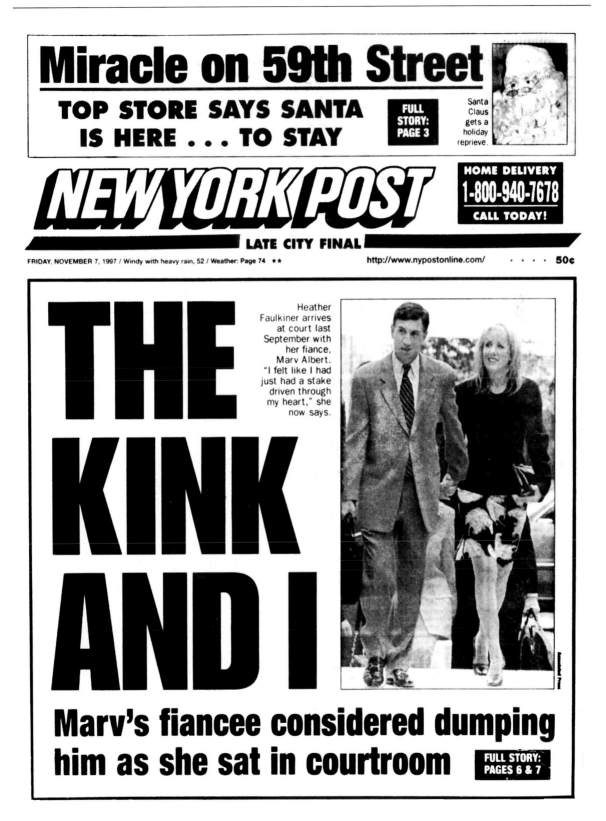

Miracle on 59th Street

TOP STORE SAYS SANTA IS HERE . . . TO STAY

FULL STORY: PAGE 3

Santa Claus gets a holiday reprieve.

NEW YORK POST

HOME DELIVERY
1-800-940-7678
CALL TODAY!

LATE CITY FINAL

FRIDAY, NOVEMBER 7, 1997 / Windy with heavy rain, 52 / Weather: Page 74 ★★   http://www.nypostonline.com/   · · · · 50¢

THE KINK AND I

Heather Faulkiner arrives at court last September with her fiance, Marv Albert. "I felt like I had just had a stake driven through my heart," she now says.

Marv's fiancee considered dumping him as she sat in courtroom

FULL STORY: PAGES 6 & 7

'Eyes' don't have it!

CRITICS RATE KUBRICK'S FINAL FILM: PAGE 38

Boss rocks Meadowlands

PAGES 4 & 5

NEW YORK POST

ONLY **50¢**

METRO EDITION

FRIDAY, JULY 16, 1999 / Sunny & hot, 93 / Weather: Page 24   http://www.nypost.com/   · 50¢

FORE PLAY

Leggy lassie stuns Tiger at Brit Open

SEE PAGE 3 AND SPORTS

A bikini-clad woman races up to embrace golfer Tiger Woods yesterday at the British Open.

City: Heat's on Con Ed again

PAGE 3

Subway crime hits all-time low

PAGE 16

Barak and Bill talk business

PAGE 2

Big losers in the tech stock rout

PAGE 2

Judge Judy: Cuban raft boy should go back

CINDY ADAMS: PAGE 12

How Jane Fonda can make comeback

PAGE 43

NEW YORK POST

ONLY 50¢

LATE CITY FINAL

FRIDAY, JANUARY 7, 2000 / Partly sunny, 50 / Weather: Page 63 ★★

http://www.nypost.com/ · · 50¢

SCREWBALL!

Atlanta Braves relief pitcher John Rocker was ordered yesterday to undergo psychiatric testing.

Baseball puts Rocker on the couch

SEE PAGE 3

Associated Press

STANDOFF
Tensions mount over U.S. spy plane in China PAGES 6 & 7

DROPOFF
City murders plummet 21% so far this year PAGE 5

CELEBRATING 200 YEARS

NEW YORK POST

25 CENTS

LATE CITY FINAL

TUESDAY. APRIL 3. 2001 / Cloudy with late showers, 52 / Weather: Page 24 ★ ★   www.nypost.com   · · 25¢

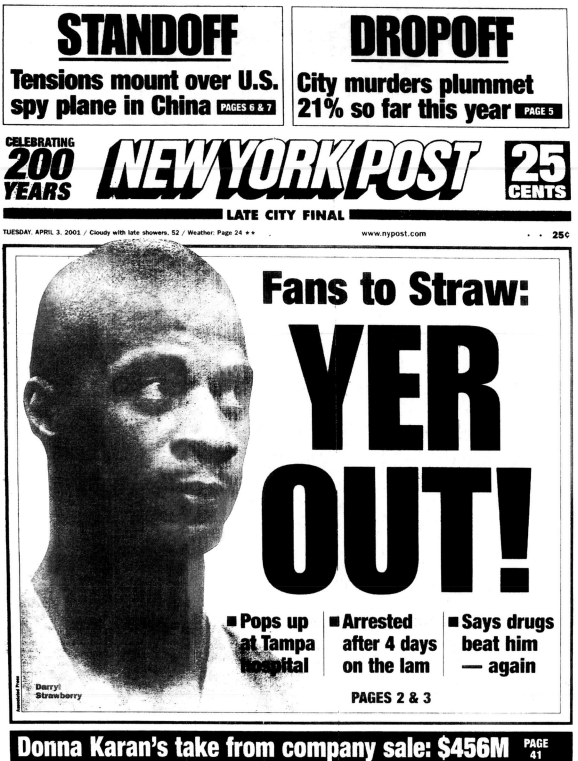

Fans to Straw:
YER OUT!

Darryl Strawberry

■ Pops up at Tampa hospital

■ Arrested after 4 days on the lam

■ Says drugs beat him — again

PAGES 2 & 3

Donna Karan's take from company sale: $456M PAGE 41

SLOPPY YANKS GET BOMBED IN SEATTLE

GEORGE KING PAGE 82

WEDNESDAY, MAY 7, 2003   R

NEW YORK POST

www.nypost.com

The Best Sports In Town®

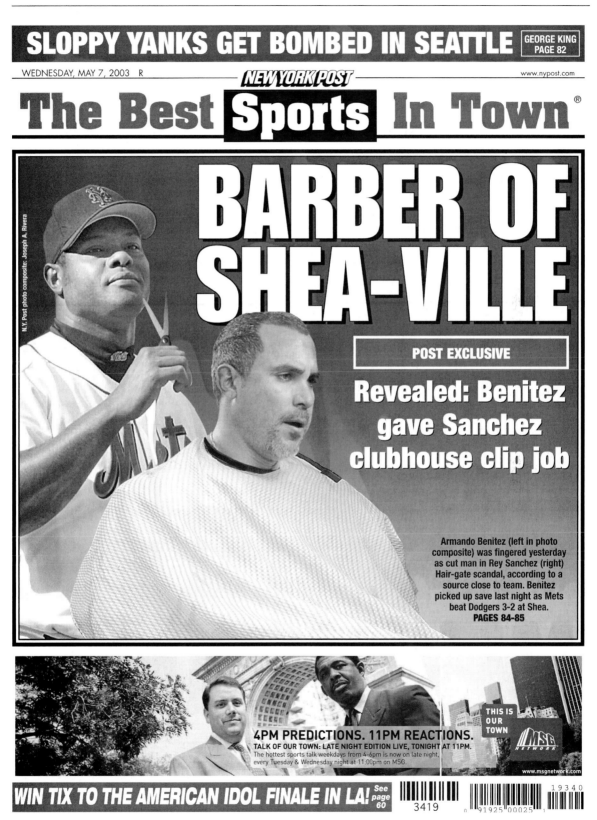

N.Y. Post photo composite: Joseph A. Rivera

BARBER OF SHEA-VILLE

POST EXCLUSIVE

Revealed: Benitez gave Sanchez clubhouse clip job

Armando Benitez (left in photo composite) was fingered yesterday as cut man in Rey Sanchez (right) Hair-gate scandal, according to a source close to team. Benitez picked up save last night as Mets beat Dodgers 3-2 at Shea.
PAGES 84-85

WIN TIX TO THE AMERICAN IDOL FINALE IN LA! *See page 60*

3419

0 91925 00025

19340

HAT TRICK
Clark hits three HRs in Yankees' rout P. 45

TOP 25
Lenn Robbins ranks college football's best P. 58-59

NEW YORK POST
SUNDAY Sports

AUGUST 29, 2004

39-PAGE PULLOUT
COVERAGE STARTS ON PAGE 37

U.S. WOMEN WIN GOLD
DETAILS / PAGE 38

American men top Lithuania for bronze

WE'RE NO. 3!

Shawn Marion heads upcourt during USA's 104-96 win over Lithuania in Olympics bronze-medal game yesterday. Win kept Americans from failing to get basketball medal for first time. MIKE VACCARO: P. 39

35710

0 91925 00050 3

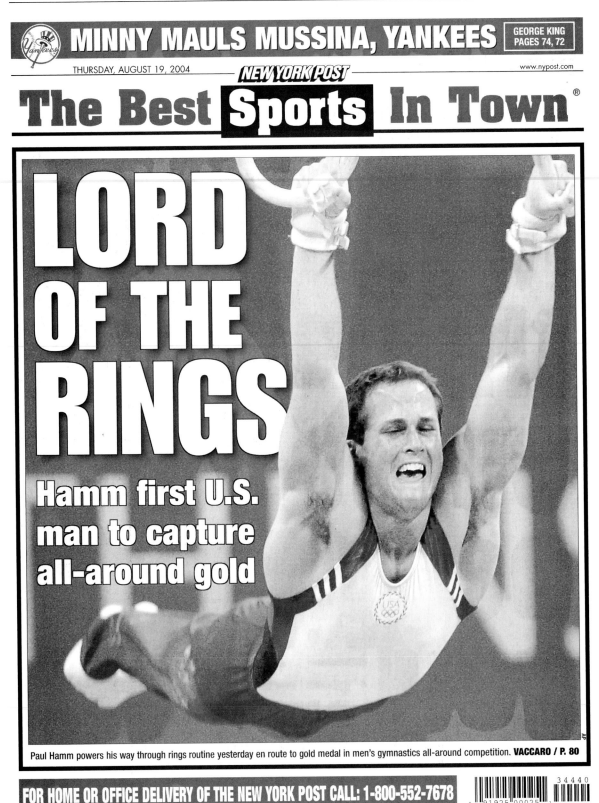

MINNY MAULS MUSSINA, YANKEES

GEORGE KING
PAGES 74, 72

THURSDAY, AUGUST 19, 2004

NEW YORK POST

www.nypost.com

The Best Sports In Town®

LORD OF THE RINGS

Hamm first U.S. man to capture all-around gold

Paul Hamm powers his way through rings routine yesterday en route to gold medal in men's gymnastics all-around competition. **VACCARO / P. 80**

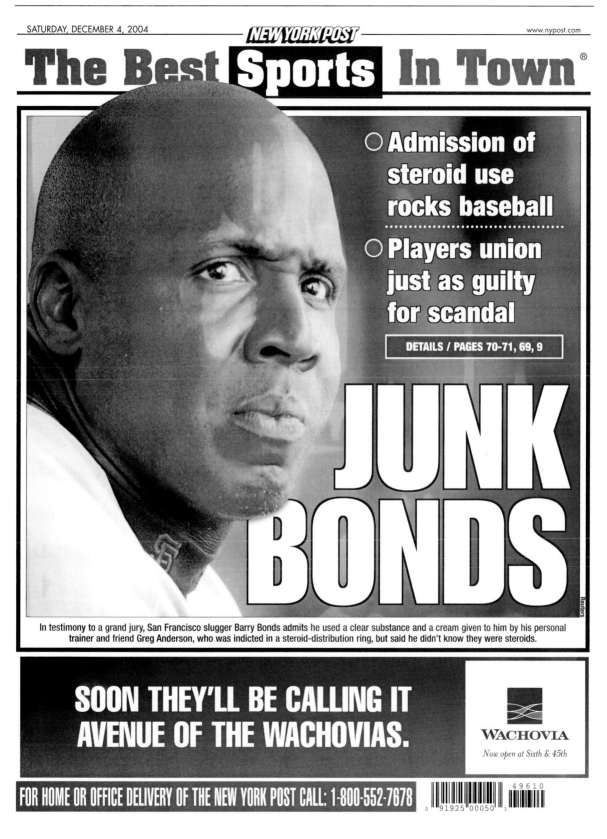

NEW YORK POST

www.nypost.com

The Best Sports In Town®

○ **Admission of steroid use rocks baseball**

○ **Players union just as guilty for scandal**

DETAILS / PAGES 70-71, 69, 9

JUNK BONDS

Reuters

In testimony to a grand jury, San Francisco slugger Barry Bonds admits he used a clear substance and a cream given to him by his personal trainer and friend Greg Anderson, who was indicted in a steroid-distribution ring, but said he didn't know they were steroids.

FOR HOME OR OFFICE DELIVERY OF THE NEW YORK POST CALL: 1-800-552-7678

49610

0 91925 00050 3

THURSDAY, MARCH 10, 2005　　NEW YORK POST　　www.nypost.com

The Best Sports In Town

CAPITOL HELL

Fired-up MLB to fight 'roid subpoenas

While Congress tried to put muscle on baseball over its steroid policy by issuing subpoenas requiring seven players, including Jason Giambi (right), to appear before a House committee, MLB vowed to challenge the legal manuever, while maintaining players could cooperate voluntarily.

PAGES 84-85

New York Post: Charles Wenzelberg

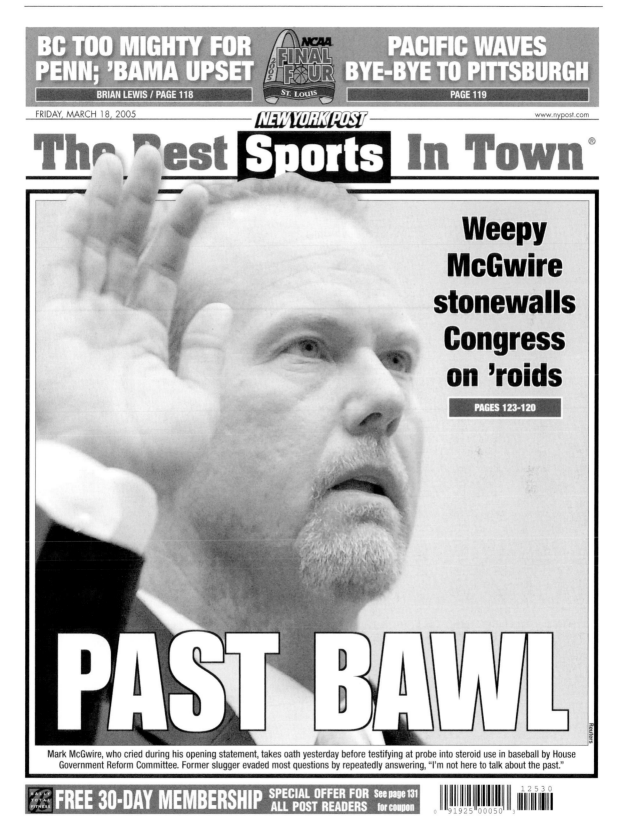

FRIDAY, MARCH 18, 2005

NEW YORK POST

www.nypost.com

The Best Sports In Town®

Weepy McGwire stonewalls Congress on 'roids

PAGES 123-120

PAST BAWL

Mark McGwire, who cried during his opening statement, takes oath yesterday before testifying at probe into steroid use in baseball by House Government Reform Committee. Former slugger evaded most questions by repeatedly answering, "I'm not here to talk about the past."

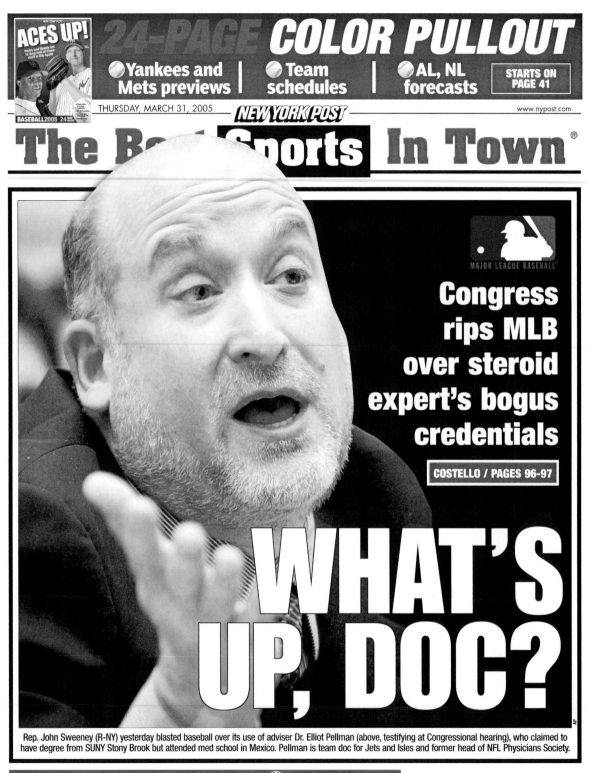

ACES UP!
Pedro and Randy set to deal Hall of Fame stuff in Big Apple

BASEBALL 2005

24-PAGE COLOR PULLOUT

⚾ Yankees and Mets previews | ⚾ Team schedules | ⚾ AL, NL forecasts | STARTS ON PAGE 41

THURSDAY, MARCH 31, 2005   *NEW YORK POST*   www.nypost.com

The Best Sports In Town®

MAJOR LEAGUE BASEBALL

Congress rips MLB over steroid expert's bogus credentials

COSTELLO / PAGES 96-97

WHAT'S UP, DOC?

Rep. John Sweeney (R-NY) yesterday blasted baseball over its use of adviser Dr. Elliot Pellman (above, testifying at Congressional hearing), who claimed to have degree from SUNY Stony Brook but attended med school in Mexico. Pellman is team doc for Jets and Isles and former head of NFL Physicians Society.

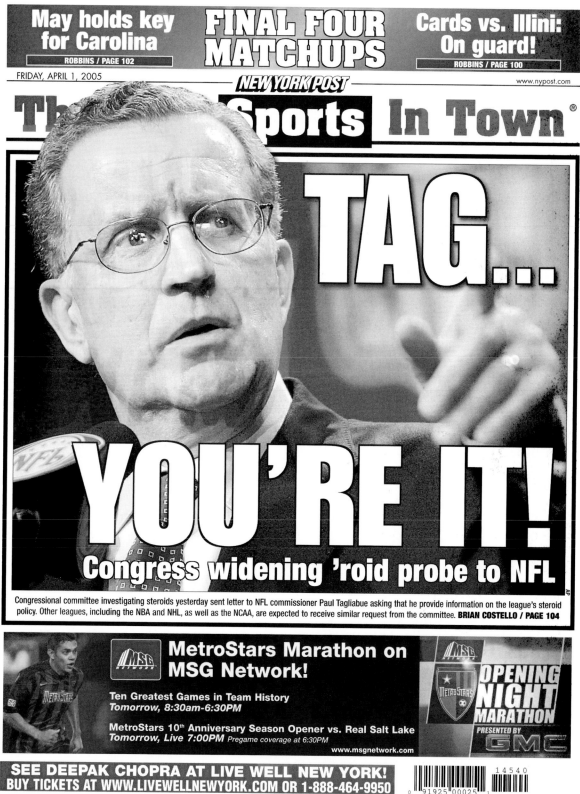

May holds key for Carolina
ROBBINS / PAGE 102

FINAL FOUR MATCHUPS

Cards vs. Illini: On guard!
ROBBINS / PAGE 100

FRIDAY, APRIL 1, 2005

NEW YORK POST

www.nypost.com

The **Sports** In Town®

TAG...
YOU'RE IT!

Congress widening 'roid probe to NFL

Congressional committee investigating steroids yesterday sent letter to NFL commissioner Paul Tagliabue asking that he provide information on the league's steroid policy. Other leagues, including the NBA and NHL, as well as the NCAA, are expected to receive similar request from the committee. **BRIAN COSTELLO / PAGE 104**

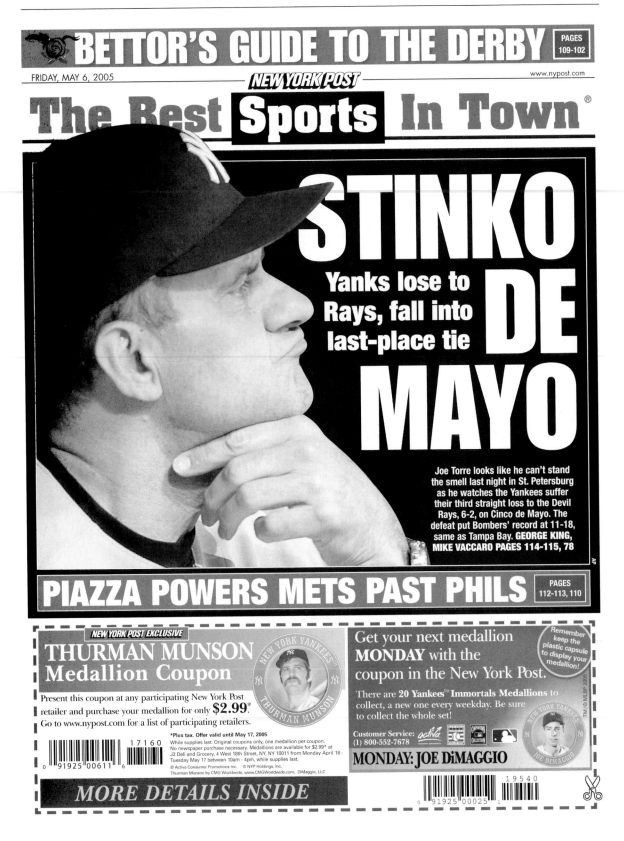

STINKO DE MAYO

Yanks lose to Rays, fall into last-place tie

Joe Torre looks like he can't stand the smell last night in St. Petersburg as he watches the Yankees suffer their third straight loss to the Devil Rays, 6-2, on Cinco de Mayo. The defeat put Bombers' record at 11-18, same as Tampa Bay. **GEORGE KING, MIKE VACCARO PAGES 114-115, 78**

PIAZZA POWERS METS PAST PHILS — PAGES 112-113, 110

LOSS TO CARDS CUTS METS TO .500
MORRISSEY, GREENBERG, GROSSMAN / PAGES 68-69, 66

MONDAY, MAY 16, 2005   *NEW YORK POST*   www.nypost.com

The Best Sports In Town®

BREW HA-HA

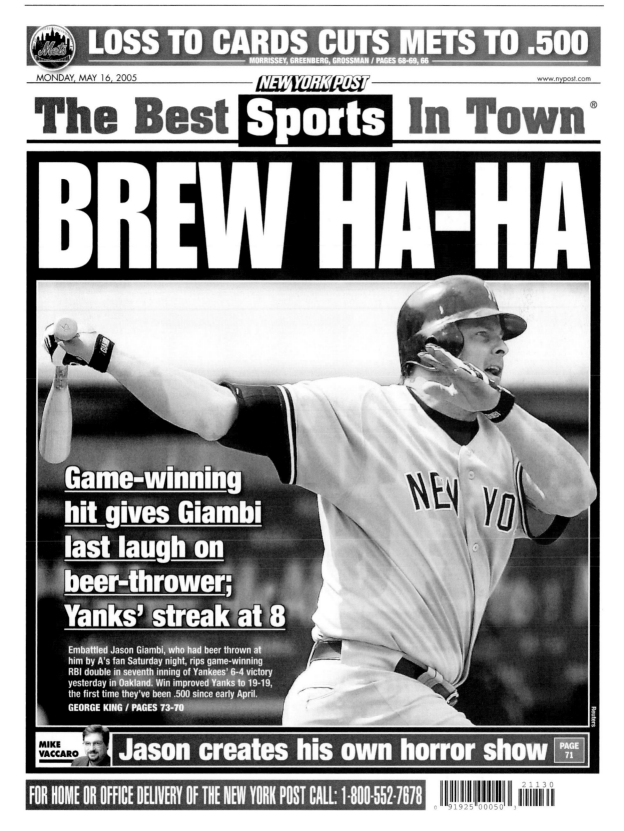

Game-winning hit gives Giambi last laugh on beer-thrower; Yanks' streak at 8

Embattled Jason Giambi, who had beer thrown at him by A's fan Saturday night, rips game-winning RBI double in seventh inning of Yankees' 6-4 victory yesterday in Oakland. Win improved Yanks to 19-19, the first time they've been .500 since early April.
GEORGE KING / PAGES 73-70

Reuters

MIKE VACCARO **Jason creates his own horror show** PAGE 71

FOR HOME OR OFFICE DELIVERY OF THE NEW YORK POST CALL: 1-800-552-7678   21130

0 91925 00050 3

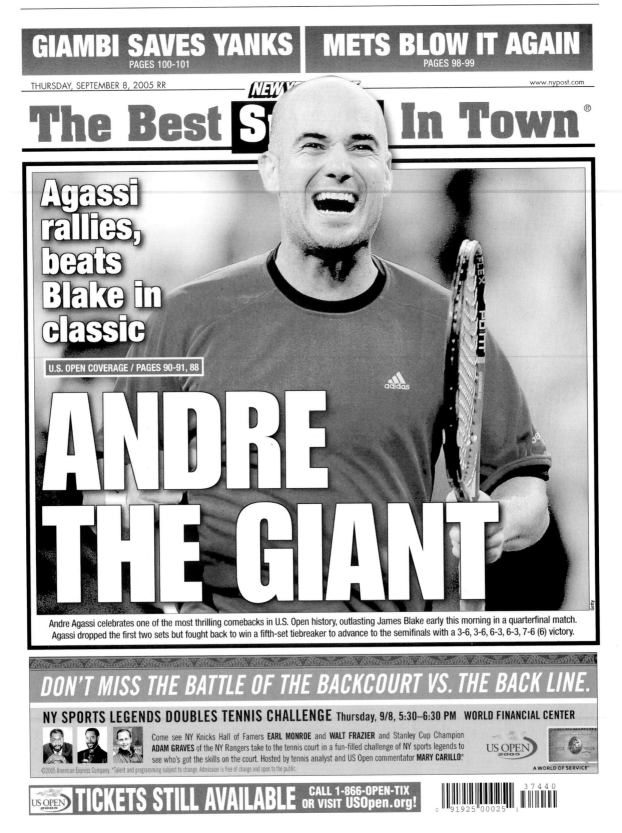

THURSDAY, SEPTEMBER 8, 2005 RR

www.nypost.com

The Best S In Town®

Agassi rallies, beats Blake in classic

U.S. OPEN COVERAGE / PAGES 90-91, 88

ANDRE THE GIANT

Andre Agassi celebrates one of the most thrilling comebacks in U.S. Open history, outlasting James Blake early this morning in a quarterfinal match. Agassi dropped the first two sets but fought back to win a fifth-set tiebreaker to advance to the semifinals with a 3-6, 3-6, 6-3, 6-3, 7-6 (6) victory.

CURRY A KNICK AS DOCS GIVE OK

BERMAN PAGE 58

SATURDAY, OCTOBER 8, 2005 — *NEW YORK POST* — www.nypost.com

The Best Sports Town®

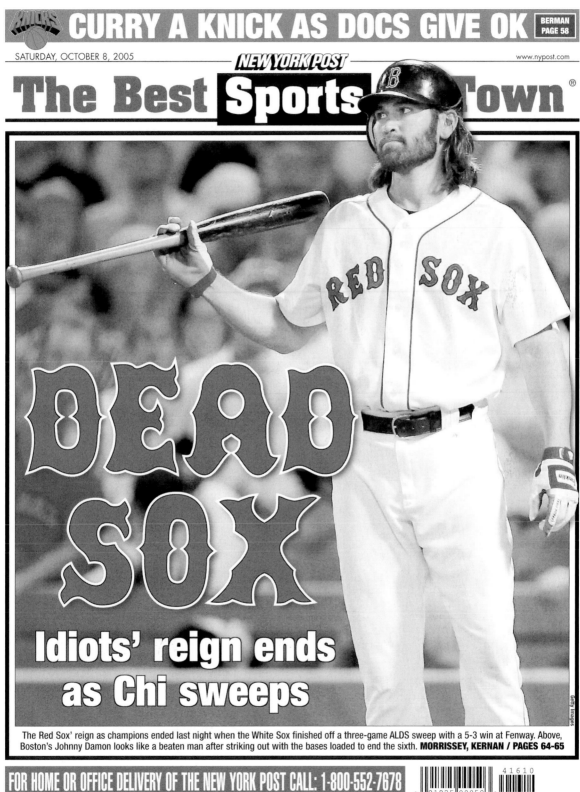

DEAD SOX

Idiots' reign ends as Chi sweeps

The Red Sox' reign as champions ended last night when the White Sox finished off a three-game ALDS sweep with a 5-3 win at Fenway. Above, Boston's Johnny Damon looks like a beaten man after striking out with the bases loaded to end the sixth. **MORRISSEY, KERNAN / PAGES 64-65**

Getty Images

41610

0 91925 00050 3

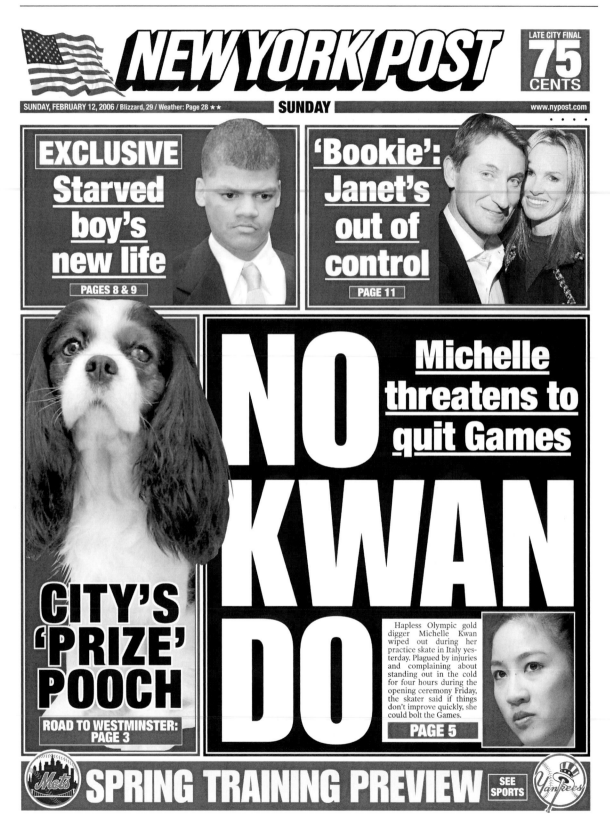

NEW YORK POST

LATE CITY FINAL
75 CENTS

SUNDAY, FEBRUARY 12, 2006 / Blizzard, 29 / Weather: Page 28 ★★   SUNDAY   www.nypost.com

EXCLUSIVE
Starved boy's new life
PAGES 8 & 9

'Bookie':
Janet's out of control
PAGE 11

NO KWAN DO

Michelle threatens to quit Games

Hapless Olympic gold digger Michelle Kwan wiped out during her practice skate in Italy yesterday. Plagued by injuries and complaining about standing out in the cold for four hours during the opening ceremony Friday, the skater said if things don't improve quickly, she could bolt the Games.
PAGE 5

CITY'S 'PRIZE' POOCH
ROAD TO WESTMINSTER: PAGE 3

SPRING TRAINING PREVIEW   SEE SPORTS

NEW YORK POST

25 CENTS

LATE CITY FINAL

WEDNESDAY, MAY 30, 2007 / Mostly sunny and very warm, 87 / Weather: Page 34 ★★   www.nypost.com • • • •   25¢

PHOTO EXCLUSIVE

STRAY-ROD
Alex hits strip club with mystery blonde

As the last-place Yankees continue their slide, superstar Alex Rodriguez and a bombshell blonde head into an elevator at the swank Four Seasons Hotel in Toronto Sunday after a night on the town — including a late-night visit to a strip joint.

PAGES 2-3

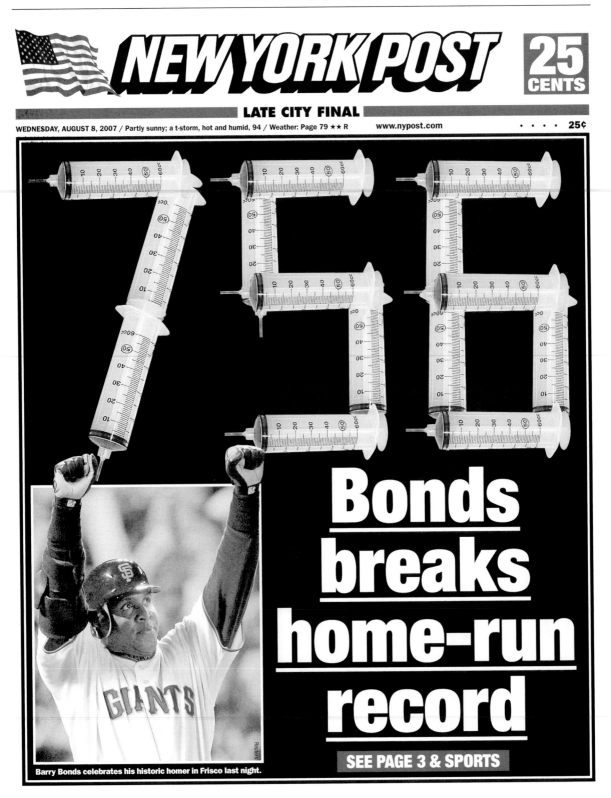

NEW YORK POST

25 CENTS

LATE CITY FINAL

WEDNESDAY, AUGUST 8, 2007 / Partly sunny; a t-storm, hot and humid, 94 / Weather: Page 79 ★★ R   www.nypost.com   • • • •   25¢

Bonds breaks home-run record

SEE PAGE 3 & SPORTS

Barry Bonds celebrates his historic homer in Frisco last night.

MAFIA

NEW YORK POST

Monday, April 14, 1986

35 CENTS

FINAL

TONIGHT: Cloudy, upper 40s.
TOMORROW: Chance of rain,
55-60. Details: Page 2.

Stock prices: P. 76
TV listings: P. 83

GOTTI #1 ON HIT PARADE

Marked for death after top aide is blown up

LATEST: PAGE 5

Courageous Crane Lady begged: 'Cut off my legs'

Walking with the aid of crutches on legs she once had pleaded with cops to 'cut off,' Brigitte Gerney arrives at Criminal Court today with her lawyers, flanked by two of her heroes, Officers Tony Mangiaracina (left) George Toth. The cops were among the rescuers who helped free her from beneath a construction crane that had crushed her last May. Mrs. Gerney gave a chilling account of the accident at the trial of the foreman in charge of the crane's operation.

DETAILS: PAGE 3

New York Post: Dan Brinzac

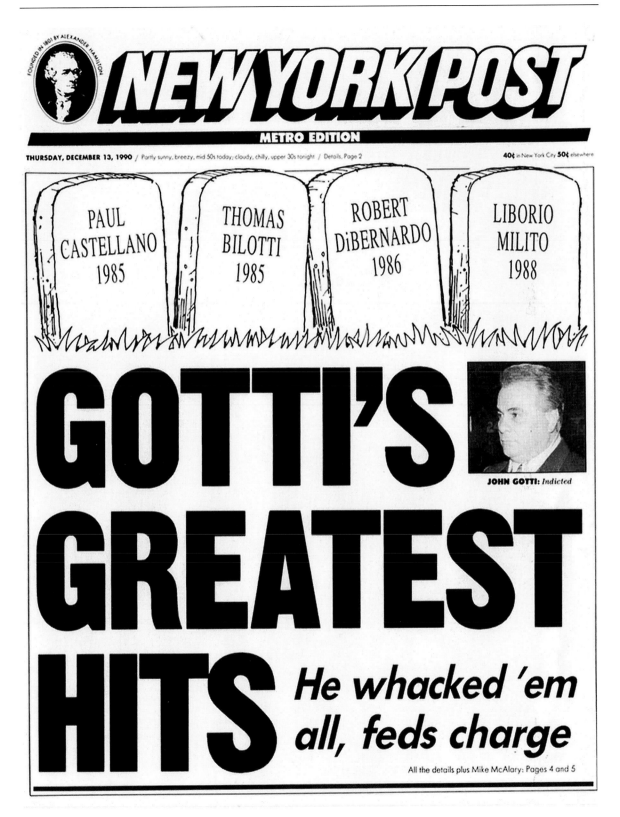

JOHN GOTTI: *Indicted*

GOTTI'S GREATEST HITS

He whacked 'em all, feds charge

All the details plus Mike McAlary: Pages 4 and 5

NEW YORK POST

25 CENTS

LATE CITY FINAL

TUESDAY, SEPTEMBER 20, 2005 / Warm and humid; a shower or t-storm, 84 / Weather: Page 62 ★★   www.nypost.com   • • • •   25¢

POST POKER

VIRGINIA SCRATCH N' WINS $250,000

BROOKLYN WOMAN SCOOPS JACKPOT

TODAY'S NUMBERS: PAGE 30

Paul Martinka

WHOOPEE! Virginia Mercuris celebrates her $250G win.

Yanks' Bubba Crosby celebrates game-winning homer last night

Hubba Bubba

SEE SPORTS

GOTTI SPLIT

Jury locked on Jr.'s mob guilt

By KATI CORNELL SMITH

Jury deliberations in the case of John "Junior" Gotti took a stunning turn yesterday as jurors revealed they are split over whether the once-powerful gangster quit the Mafia — raising the specter of a mistrial.

Gotti's eyes welled with tears of relief as Manhattan federal

See **GOTTI** Page 4

Teflon Son

Not since the fictional Vito Corleone of *The Godfather* had New York seen a mobster like John Gotti. He wore natty clothes, reveled in public attention and basked in the adoration of his neighbors, whom he befriended with (illegal) holiday fireworks shows. He even talked to reporters. The "Dapper Don"—as he was referred to by *The Post*—became a public fixture of sorts in the mid-1980s with his $10,000 hand-tailored Brioni suits and headline-grabbing antics.

Gotti received another—perhaps more memorable—media nickname when he twice beat racketeering charges brought against him. The feds weren't able to make their case stick, and Gotti was now the "Teflon Don."

So, in 2005, when John Gotti Jr. was acquitted on charges of fraud, *The Post*'s headline was inevitable: Gotti Jr. was the "Teflon Son."

The label, like all things Mafia, stayed in the family.

The Oddfather

Of all the mob figures who have appeared on *The Post*'s front page—from Dutch Schultz to Meyer Lansky to Joe Columbo to Joey Gallo to John Gotti—none has been as bizarre as Vincent "Chin" Gigante, whom the paper christened "The Oddfather."

A onetime pro boxer turned mob hit man (he famously botched a 1957 hit on the boss of all bosses, Frank Costello), Gigante quietly rose through the ranks to become boss of the Genovese family in 1981—although for five years he allowed Anthony "Fat Tony" Salerno to pose as the boss in order to deflect attention.

Once he was ID'd as the real head of the family, though, Gigante put on a public spectacle the likes of which had never before been seen: He took to wandering the streets of Little Italy in a bathrobe, disheveled and unshaven,

mumbling to himself or whoever was holding his arm. The feds were convinced it was all a ruse and indicted him in 1990 on racketeering and murder charges.

But Gigante put on too good an act, and it was seven years before the government could even bring him to trial. When it did, it was only because such mob rats as Sammy "The Bull" Gravano and Phil Leonetti broke the code of silence and testified that a fully lucid Gigante had given them orders to kill during the time he was supposedly mentally ill.

A jury convicted Gigante on numerous counts and he received a 12-year prison term. In 2003, however, after being indicted on separate charges, he agreed to a plea bargain under which he finally admitted that the whole Oddfather routine had been just that. Gigante died in prison in 2005 at the age of 78.

NEW YORK POST

METRO EDITION

THURSDAY, MARCH 12, 1992 / Partly sunny, mid 30s today; clear, low in the 20s tonight / Details, Page 2   40¢ in New York City 50¢ elsewhere

Sammy the Bull chopped brother-in-law up into little pieces and had him . . .

FED TO THE DOGS

Mob turncoat Sammy "The Bull" Gravano killed his brother-in-law Nick Scibetta and scattered his remains in an area where dogs roam, it was disclosed in Brooklyn Federal Court yesterday at the trial of John Gotti. Only one body part was recovered for burial — a hand that had been dug up by a family pet. Gravano attended the funeral but never let on he was responsible for the murder.

The latest on the John Gotti trial: Page Four

WRESTLING HIT BY GAY SEX SCANDAL

Tales of teenage boys being abused on the circuit: Page 7

NUDE PIX SMEAR OF EX-PRINCIPAL

She says it's because she blew whistle on corruption: Page 5

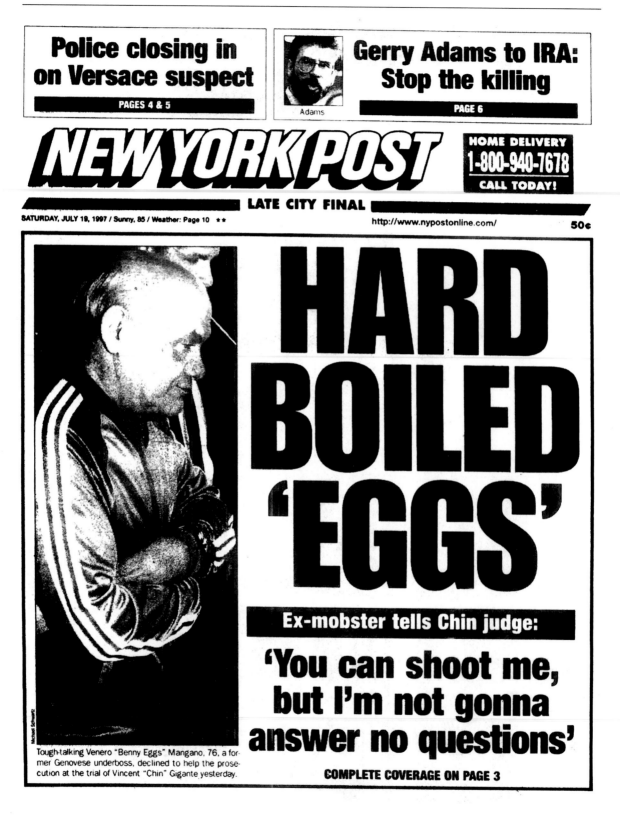

NEW YORK POST

HOME DELIVERY
1-800-940-7678
CALL TODAY!

LATE CITY FINAL

SATURDAY, JULY 19, 1997 / Sunny, 85 / Weather: Page 10 ★★

http://www.nypostonline.com/

50¢

HARD BOILED 'EGGS'

Ex-mobster tells Chin judge:

'You can shoot me, but I'm not gonna answer no questions'

Tough-talking Venero "Benny Eggs" Mangano, 76, a former Genovese underboss, declined to help the prosecution at the trial of Vincent "Chin" Gigante yesterday.

COMPLETE COVERAGE ON PAGE 3

NEW YORK POST

25 CENTS

LATE CITY FINAL

THURSDAY, MAY 1, 2003 / Cloudy & breezy; possible shower, 69 / Weather: Page 40 ★★   www.nypost.com   · · · · **25¢**

FAIRY GODFATHER

Mob trial sensation

Mafia boss whacked for being gay

A Mafia turncoat told a stunned courtroom yesterday he executed mob boss John D'Amato — because D'Amato was gay and the DeCavalcante family feared becoming the laughingstock of the underworld.

"Nobody's gonna respect us if we have a gay homosexual boss sitting down discussing La Cosa Nostra business," Anthony Capo told jurors in Manhattan federal court.

FULL STORY: PAGE 7

Thugs said "Johnny Boy" D'Amato shamed the family.

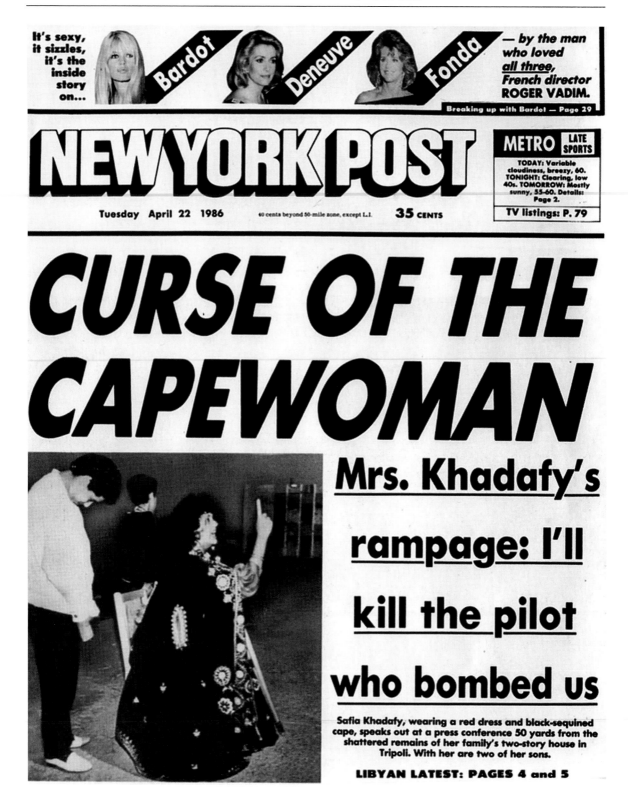

It's sexy, it sizzles, it's the inside story on... **Bardot** **Deneuve** **Fonda** — by the man who loved *all three*, French director ROGER VADIM.

Breaking up with Bardot — Page 29

NEW YORK POST

Tuesday   April 22   1986   40 cents beyond 50-mile zone, except L.I.   **35 CENTS**

METRO LATE SPORTS
TODAY: Variable cloudiness, breezy, 60. TONIGHT: Clearing, low 40s. TOMORROW: Mostly sunny, 55-60. Details: Page 2.
TV listings: P. 79

CURSE OF THE CAPEWOMAN

Mrs. Khadafy's rampage: I'll kill the pilot who bombed us

Safia Khadafy, wearing a red dress and black-sequined cape, speaks out at a press conference 50 yards from the shattered remains of her family's two-story house in Tripoli. With her are two of her sons.

LIBYAN LATEST: PAGES 4 and 5

NEW YORK POST

Tuesday   June 17   1986

40 cents beyond 50-mile zone, except L.I.

35 CENTS

METRO · TODAY'S RACING

TODAY: Breezy, sunny, 80. TONIGHT: Clear, mid 50s. TOMORROW: Sunny, mid 70s. Details: Page 2.

TV listings: P. 79

KHADAFY GOES DAFFY

He's turned into a transvestite druggie

PAGE FOUR

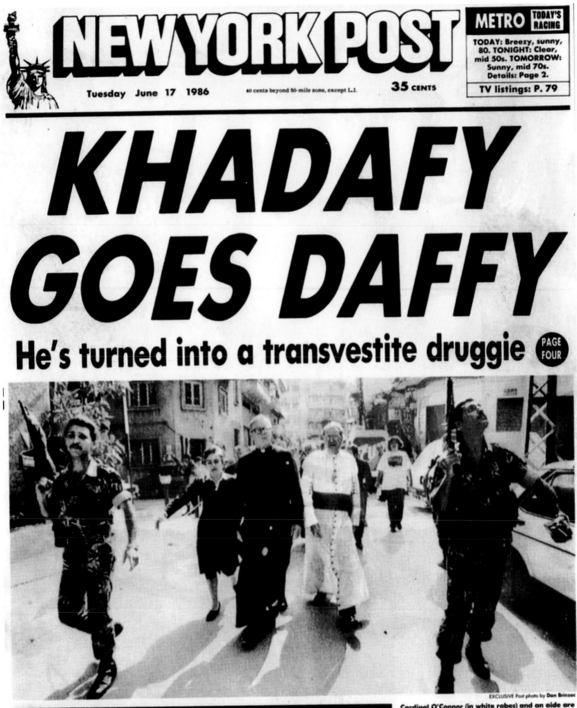

EXCLUSIVE Post photo by Dan Brinzac

Cardinal in Leb war zone

Cardinal O'Connor (in white robes) and an aide are escorted by heavily armed police en route to a meeting in dangerous West Beirut which could lead to the release of 22 hostages — five of them Americans — held by Lebanese militants. *PAGE 4*

Gen. Manuel Noriega is shackled by DEA agents aboard military plane and as he appeared for mugshot in Miami yesterday. PAGES 4 and 5.

Canned Pineapple

It was humiliating enough for Panamanian dictator Manuel Noriega to be toppled from power in 1989 by a U.S. invading force and placed on trial in Miami for drug trafficking.

But talk about rubbing salt in the wound: *The Post*'s Page One played off Noriega's famous nickname, "Pineapple Face," which he got thanks to his notoriously pockmarked complexion.

Ever since Noriega's 1988 indictment on cocaine trafficking and money-laundering charges, the first Bush administration had pressed Noriega to step down and stand trial, but he refused. A year later, when a U.S. marine was murdered on the streets of Panama City, troops were sent in.

Noriega took refuge at the Vatican embassy in Panama's capital. In response, U.S. troops stationed outside blasted rock music—particularly the Van Halen song "Panama"—through loudspeakers in a form of psychological warfare. Eventually, he surrendered and was flown to Miami, where he was convicted and sentenced to 30 years in prison.

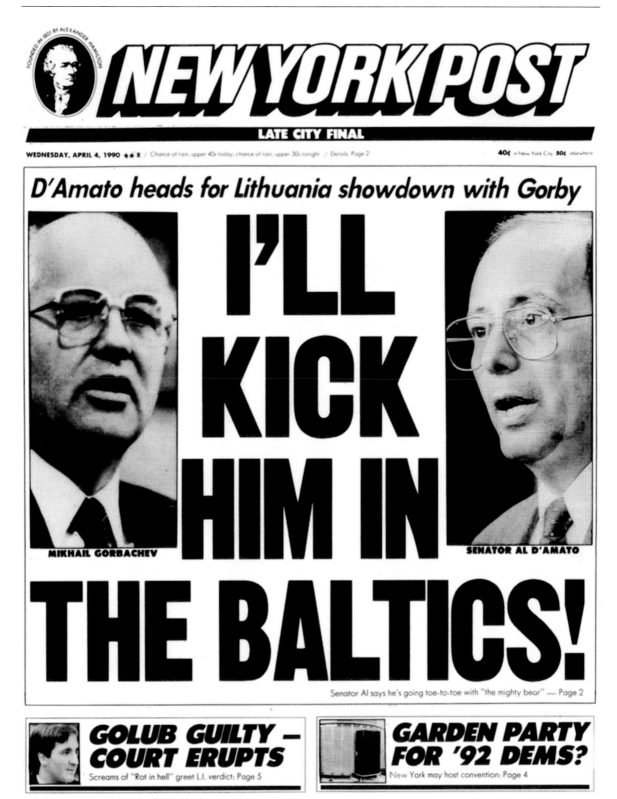

FOUNDED IN 1801 BY ALEXANDER HAMILTON

NEW YORK POST

LATE CITY FINAL

WEDNESDAY, APRIL 4, 1990 ★★ R / Chance of rain, upper 40s today; chance of rain, upper 30s tonight / Details, Page 2

40¢ in New York City 50¢ elsewhere

D'Amato heads for Lithuania showdown with Gorby

I'LL KICK HIM IN THE BALTICS!

MIKHAIL GORBACHEV

SENATOR AL D'AMATO

Senator Al says he's going toe-to-toe with "the mighty bear" — Page 2

GOLUB GUILTY — COURT ERUPTS
Screams of "Rot in hell" greet L.I. verdict: Page 5

GARDEN PARTY FOR '92 DEMS?
New York may host convention: Page 4

FOUNDED IN 1801 BY ALEXANDER HAMILTON

NEW YORK POST

METRO EDITION

THURSDAY, AUGUST 22, 1991 / Sunny, mid 80s today; clear, mid 60s tonight / Details, Page 2

40¢ in New York City **50¢** elsewhere

GORBY'S BACK!

- **Coup crumbles, plotters on the run**
- **Freed Mikhail returns to Moscow**
- **Jubilant Soviets celebrate freedom**

HISTORIC DAY IN THE SOVIET UNION: PAGES 4 AND 5

ECKED: survey l car on Eastern rkway rioters turned ng the day of protests in Crown Heights.

New York Post: Kevin Cohen

ANOTHER NIGHT OF VIOLENCE IN B'KLYN

Race riots rock Crown Heights: Pages 2 and 3

LATE CITY FINAL

WEDNESDAY, SEPTEMBER 2, 1992 / Sunny, 70s today; fair, 60s tonight / Details, Page 2 ★★

40¢ in New York City 50¢ elsewhere

A book by a former member of the Buckingham Palace staff paints a different picture of life with Queen Elizabeth and her royal family than their majestic public image.

POST EXCLUSIVE

Tell-all book Queen doesn't want you to read

ROYAL FOOLS

A look inside private life at Buckingham Palace . . .

CINDY ADAMS

All the juicy details: Page 5

MARTINA SURVIVES 1st ROUND SCARE

Exciting action at the U.S. Open: Pages 43-45

SAMMY THE BULL RATS ON GOTTI JR.

EXCLUSIVE

Page 3

GOTTI JR.   GRAVANO

NEW YORK POST

LATE CITY FINAL

TUESDAY, OCTOBER 18, 1994 / Partly sunny today, low 60s; cloudy tonight, near 45 / Details, Page 24 ★★

50¢

DI-VORCE

Princess to get $35M in final split, says book

Page 3

SPLITSVILLE: *New book reports royal couple (pictured here in 1985) will divorce next year.*

Giants coach to QB: Produce or you're out   Pages 70 & 71

4 cops face charges in drug dealer shakedowns

EXCLUSIVE: PAGE 5

Top pol favors pay hikes for state officeholders

EXCLUSIVE: PAGE 9

NEW YORK POST

METRO EDITION

WEDNESDAY, SEPTEMBER 4, 1996 / Partly cloudy, 82 / Weather: Page 43   http://www.nypostonline.com/   · · 50¢

HE'S SADDAM MAD!

Iraqi boss vows revenge for U.S. missile attack

Iraqi strongman Saddam Hussein takes to the airwaves yesterday in Baghdad to condemn the American missile attack.

COMPLETE COVERAGE BEGINS ON PAGE 2

Associated Press

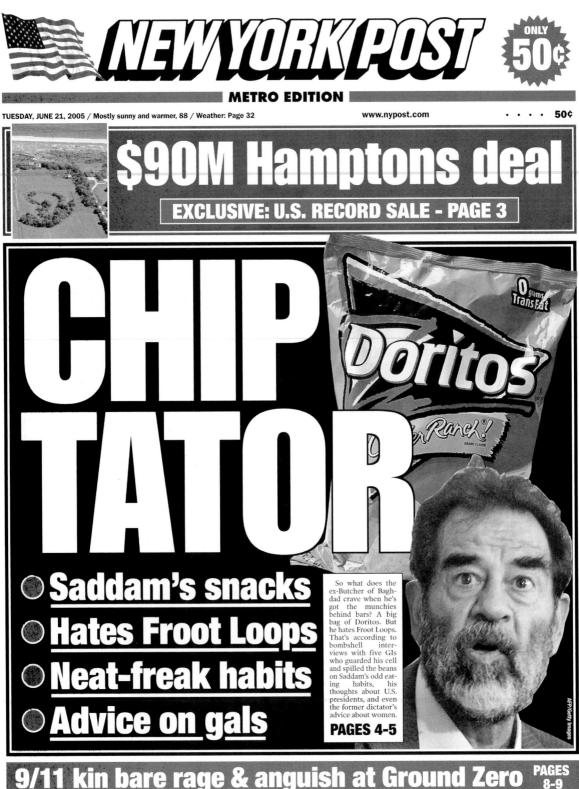

NEW YORK POST

ONLY 50¢

METRO EDITION

TUESDAY, JUNE 21, 2005 / Mostly sunny and warmer, 88 / Weather: Page 32   www.nypost.com   · · · ·   50¢

$90M Hamptons deal
EXCLUSIVE: U.S. RECORD SALE - PAGE 3

CHIP TATOR

- **Saddam's snacks**
- **Hates Froot Loops**
- **Neat-freak habits**
- **Advice on gals**

So what does the ex-Butcher of Baghdad crave when he's got the munchies behind bars? A big bag of Doritos. But he hates Froot Loops. That's according to bombshell interviews with five GIs who guarded his cell and spilled the beans on Saddam's odd eating habits, his thoughts about U.S. presidents, and even the former dictator's advice about women.

PAGES 4-5

AFP/Getty Images

9/11 kin bare rage & anguish at Ground Zero
PAGES 8-9

NEW YORK POST

25 CENTS

LATE CITY FINAL

MONDAY, NOVEMBER 6, 2006 / Sun and clouds, 58 / Weather: Page 34 ★★ R   www.nypost.com   • • • • 25¢

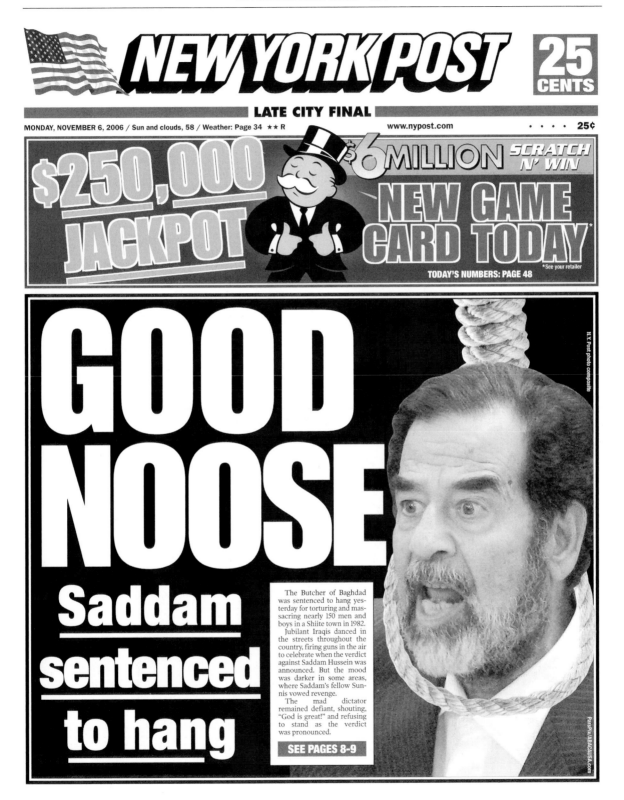

N.Y. Post photo composite

PataPix/ABACAUSA.com

GOOD NOOSE

Saddam sentenced to hang

The Butcher of Baghdad was sentenced to hang yesterday for torturing and massacring nearly 150 men and boys in a Shiite town in 1982.

Jubilant Iraqis danced in the streets throughout the country, firing guns in the air to celebrate when the verdict against Saddam Hussein was announced. But the mood was darker in some areas, where Saddam's fellow Sunnis vowed revenge.

The mad dictator remained defiant, shouting, "God is great!" and refusing to stand as the verdict was pronounced.

SEE PAGES 8-9

CELEBRATING **200 YEARS**

NEW YORK POST

25 CENTS

LATE CITY FINAL

TUESDAY, DECEMBER 11, 2001 / Cloudy, chance of showers, 53 / Weather: Page 34   www.nypost.com   · · · · **25¢**

BOMBS 'Я' US

Hooded Palestinians in full Hamas suicide-bomber gear send a message of terror to the world by strapping fake explosives around a child's waist.   Getty Images

Terror thugs groom future suicide killers

By BILL HOFFMANN

This shocking photo shows a little Palestinian boy, who should be playing with toys, being cruelly robbed of his childhood.

He and other kids — as young as 4 and no older than 8 — are fitted with fake explosives as they are taught how to become suicidal terrorists by members of the Palestinian terror group Hamas.

These classes of hate, which were held over the weekend, were part of the 14th anniversary celebration of Hamas in Ain El Helweh, the largest Palestinian refugee camp in Lebanon.

Hamas has claimed responsibility for recent suicide bombings in Israel that have claimed 25 lives.

Followers say it's an honor to die as a martyr to their cause— an ideal drummed into their heads at a very early age.

That's evident in these exercises, in which about 40 boys were lined up and fitted with empty explosives canisters.

Then, hooded Hamas members — many of them the boys' fathers — showed them the

See **BOMBERS** Page 2

200 YEARS

NEW YORK POST

HOME DELIVERY
1-800-552-7678
CALL TODAY!

▌LATE CITY FINAL▐

MONDAY, DECEMBER 17, 2001 / Rainy, 50 / Weather: Page 32   www.nypost.com   • • • •   50¢

SEE YA LATER AL QAEDA

Last terror stronghold falls as Osama hunt goes on

Defense Secretary Donald Rumsfeld rallies the troops at Bagram Airfield during a surprise trip to Kabul yesterday.

AP

By CHRIS TOMLINSON
in Tora Bora
and JOHN LEHMANN *in N.Y.*

The al Qaeda terror network in Afghanistan is dead, but Osama bin Laden is still on the run. An international hunt for the world's most wanted man was under way last night after al Qaeda's mountain lair at Tora Bora was routed following two months of relentless U.S. bombing.

The victory came as Secretary of Defense Donald Rumsfeld became the most senior American official to visit Afghanistan in 25 years when he made a surprise trip to Kabul to meet with Hamid Karzai, head of the interim Afghan government.

Jubilant Afghans celebrated with chants of "Al Qaeda is finished! Al Qaeda is fin- ished!" as eastern-alliance military chief Haji Zaman declared, "This is the last day of al Qaeda in Afghanistan."

The successful campaign to free Afghanistan of terrorists also triggered an unexpected concession, with former Tal-

See **AL QAEDA** *Page 2*

Arafat calls for halt to attacks on Israel: Pages 6 & 7

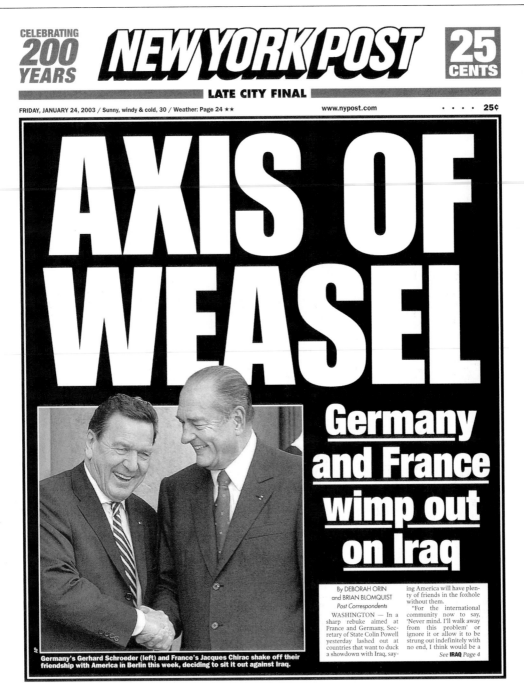

NEW YORK POST

LATE CITY FINAL

FRIDAY, JANUARY 24, 2003 / Sunny, windy & cold, 30 / Weather: Page 24 ★★   www.nypost.com   · · · ·   **25¢**

25 CENTS

AXIS OF WEASEL

Germany and France wimp out on Iraq

By DEBORAH ORIN
and BRIAN BLOMQUIST

Post Correspondents

WASHINGTON — In a sharp rebuke aimed at France and Germany, Secretary of State Colin Powell yesterday lashed out at countries that want to duck a showdown with Iraq, say-ing America will have plenty of friends in the foxhole without them.

"For the international community now to say, 'Never mind. I'll walk away from this problem' or ignore it or allow it to be strung out indefinitely with no end, I think would be a

See **IRAQ** *Page 4*

Germany's Gerhard Schroeder (left) and France's Jacques Chirac shake off their friendship with America in Berlin this week, deciding to sit it out against Iraq.

Axis of Weasel

When it comes to headlines, sometimes they come from the most unlikely sources.

With "Axis of Weasel," that source was Joe Cunningham—now a desk man but then a mere copy kid.

Like a lot of the better ones, "Axis of Weasel" was collaborative. A couple of headline writers were kicking around "Axis of something"; but it was Joe who nailed it down.

CELEBRATING 200 YEARS

NEW YORK POST

25 CENTS

LATE CITY FINAL

FRIDAY, FEBRUARY 14, 2003 / Mostly sunny, 32 / Weather: Page 38 ★★   www.nypost.com   • • • •   25¢

U.N. MEETS

FRANCE

SECRETARY-GENERAL

PRESIDENT

GERMANY

Post photo composite by Dennis Wickman

Weasels to hear
new Iraq evidence

By DEBORAH ORIN
and BRIAN BLOMQUIST
Post Correspondents

WASHINGTON — Weasel so-called allies France and Germany will hear fresh evidence today of Iraqi stonewalling, at an 11th-hour showdown with the United States in the U.N. Security Council.

As chief weapons inspector Hans Blix gives his final report, Secretary of State Colin Powell has vowed to confront the

See **WEASELS** *Page 6*

Anyway, it was perfect, resonating with the public (and a *lot* of other news outlets) from the get-go.

The line then took on a life of its own.

Days later, *The Post* came up with equally bold "U.N. Meets" front page. It was another hit.

NEW YORK POST

25 CENTS

LATE CITY FINAL

THURSDAY, NOVEMBER 11, 2004 / Partly sunny; a milder afternoon, 60 / Weather: Page 81 ★★   www.nypost.com   · · · · **25¢**

ARAFAT DEAD

And he won't be missed

FULL STORY: PAGES 2 & 3

Nanny nails Danny — Pelosi trial bombshell PAGES 6-7

NEW YORK POST

25 CENTS

LATE CITY FINAL

THURSDAY, DECEMBER 23, 2004 / Heavy rain moving in; windy, mild, foggy, 57 / Weather: Page 32 ★★ www.nypost.com • • • •   25¢

Why I split from Rudy
FULL STORY: PAGE 7

Arafat's N.Y. cash secret

BOWLING FOR PALESTINE

Terror big's $1.3M in Village biz

Bowlmor Lanes

Terror chief Yasser Arafat pumped $1.3 million into the famed Bowlmor Lanes in the heart of Greenwich Village, according to a shocking new report. The late Palestinian leader and notorious terrorist invested in the bowling center through a front company he set up in Delaware.

The news that Arafat was looking to grow his Palestinian cash stash via Bowlmor stunned bowlers there yesterday, as well as the founder of the lanes, who said he had no idea that he received Arafat's cash.

Bowlmor is renowned as a celebrity hot spot, which has hosted former Mayor Rudy Giuliani, actress Cameron Diaz and countless bar mitzvah and bat mitzvah parties.

FULL STORY: PAGE 5

Post photo composite

NEW YORK POST

25 CENTS

LATE CITY FINAL

FRIDAY, JANUARY 14, 2005 / Windy; rain for a time, colder late, 57 / Weather: Page 32 ★★   www.nypost.com   • • • • **25¢**

Getty Images

Der Furor
Raging Charles orders 'Nazi Harry' to tour Auschwitz

FULL STORY: PAGES 8-9

©THE SUN

Prince Harry wears a Nazi uniform to a party, creating an international outrage.

Oscar rip-off fight
PAGE 3

RACE FIX
Gambler doping scandal shocks Big A, Belmont

A national racing scandal is brewing as the feds probe allegations of horse doping and illegal betting at major tracks in New York, Florida and California. Seventeen people were busted yesterday on charges of operating a mob-connected ring that doped horses at Aqueduct and Belmont and allowed high rollers to place bets via the Internet. But lawmen say that's just the tip of the iceberg and a whole slew of further arrests will follow.

FULL STORY: PAGES 4-5

NEW YORK POST

LATE CITY FINAL

25 CENTS

WEDNESDAY, FEBRUARY 9, 2005 / Becoming cloudy, 52 / Weather: Page 102 ★★   www.nypost.com   • • • • 25¢

24-page Tempo pullout inside

Rock's top rich list PAGE 19

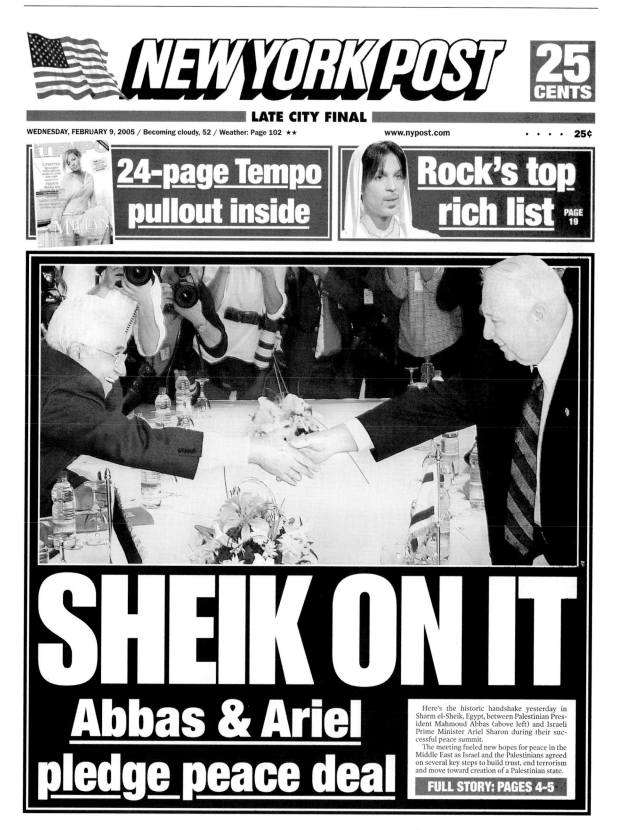

SHEIK ON IT
Abbas & Ariel pledge peace deal

Here's the historic handshake yesterday in Sharm el-Sheik, Egypt, between Palestinian President Mahmoud Abbas (above left) and Israeli Prime Minister Ariel Sharon during their successful peace summit.

The meeting fueled new hopes for peace in the Middle East as Israel and the Palestinians agreed on several key steps to build trust, end terrorism and move toward creation of a Palestinian state.

FULL STORY: PAGES 4-5

NEW YORK POST

ONLY 50¢

METRO EDITION

MONDAY, JULY 25, 2005 / An a.m. t-shower, partly sunny, 92 / Weather: Page 24

www.nypost.com

· · · · 50¢

WATER RATS

Mirrorpix

Subway terror fiends took holiday before massacre

Suicide bombers Mohammad Sidique Khan, flashing a peace sign, and Shehzad Tanweer, front right, were all smiles as they whitewater-rafted in Wales a month before carrying out the July 7 terror attacks in London that claimed 52 lives. Authorities say the bombers responsible for last Thursday's aborted attacks were on the same trip.

FULL STORY: PAGE 6

Benson sharp as Mets shut out Dodgers 6-0 SEE SPORTS

HOME DELIVERY
1-800-552-7678
CALL TODAY!

NEW YORK POST

LATE CITY FINAL

SATURDAY, JULY 30, 2005 / Clouds, some sun and a shower around, 85 / Weather: Page 26 ★★   www.nypost.com   · · · · 50¢

$10,000 WINNER
Maurice scoops Scratch & Win cash
PAGE 3

Al Qa-ught

Two of the failed bombers, Muktar Ibrahim (left) and Ramsi Mohammed, stand in their undies and raise hands in surrender yesterday after a London siege.

ZUMA Press

Cops catch five London bombers

All five al Qaeda-linked suspects in the failed London transit bombings have been nabbed in raids that spanned from England to Rome.

Two suspects were captured yesterday in London after being ordered to strip on a balcony of their apartment, and a third was arrested a mile away.

A fourth subway-bomb suspect was grabbed yesterday in Rome, and another was picked up two days ago in England.

FULL STORY: PAGES 4-5

NEW YORK POST

METRO EDITION

ONLY 50¢

MONDAY, NOVEMBER 14, 2005 / A mix of sun and clouds, 64 / Weather: Page 40   www.nypost.com   · · · · 50¢

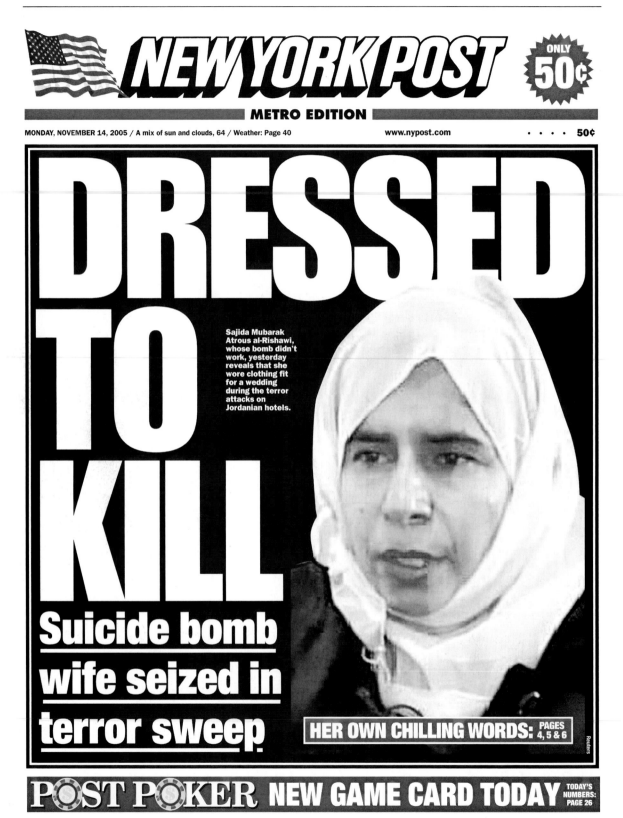

DRESSED TO KILL

Sajida Mubarak Atrous al-Rishawi, whose bomb didn't work, yesterday reveals that she wore clothing fit for a wedding during the terror attacks on Jordanian hotels.

Suicide bomb wife seized in terror sweep

HER OWN CHILLING WORDS: PAGES 4, 5 & 6

Reuters

POST POKER NEW GAME CARD TODAY TODAY'S NUMBERS: PAGE 26

The bloodied corpse of terror fiend Abu Musab al-Zarqawi lies in Iraq yesterday after U.S. bombers blasted the al Qaeda leader's "safe" house.

HOW AMERICA KILLED A MASTER TERRORIST FULL COVERAGE: PAGES 2-10

LATE CITY FINAL

THURSDAY, JUNE 7, 2007 / Plenty of sunshine, 81 / Weather: Page 42 ★★   www.nypost.com   • • • •   25¢

COME TO PAPA!

Lunatic hurls self at pope

FULL STORY: PAGE 7

Gang's back for 'Ocean's Thirteen'
REVIEW: PAGE 45

NEW YORK POST

25 CENTS

LATE CITY FINAL

TUESDAY, JUNE 19, 2007 / Partly sunny, hot and more humid, 94 / Weather: Page 38 ★★   www.nypost.com   • • • •   25¢

Piece in the Mideast

Maxim magazine

Hebrew-haha over Israeli beauty queen PAGE 3

Tiger and wife, Elin. Icon SMI

It's a cub for new dad Tiger
SEE PAGE 3

FREE CASH

$25 to attend school, $200 to visit doc

Poor kids and their parents will pocket cash rewards — from $25 for good school attendance to $200 for visiting the doctor to $3,000 for passing five Regents exams — under an anti-poverty program unveiled by city officials yesterday.

SEE PAGE 2